DO YOU DARE TRUST GOD
FOR YOUR FAMILY SIZE?

POSITIVELY YES!

DO YOU DARE TRUST GOD
FOR YOUR FAMILY SIZE?

POSITIVELY YES!

HANNA E. FARWELL

© 2006 by Hanna E. Farwell. All rights reserved.

Pleasant Word (a division of WinePress Publishing, PO Box 428, Enumclaw, WA 98022) functions only as book publisher. As such, the ultimate design, content, editorial accuracy, and views expressed or implied in this work are those of the author.

No part of this publication may be reproduced, stored in a retrieval system or transmitted in any way by any means—electronic, mechanical, photocopy, recording or otherwise—without the prior permission of the copyright holder, except as provided by USA copyright law.

Unless otherwise noted, all Scriptures are taken from the Holy Bible, New International Version, Copyright © 1973, 1978, 1984 by the International Bible Society. Used by permission of Zondervan Publishing House. The "NIV" and "New International Version" trademarks are registered in the United States Patent and Trademark Office by International Bible Society.

ISBN 1-4141-0565-7
Library of Congress Catalog Card Number: 2005907962

Dedication

This book is dedicated to you, the reader, and to your children –may you be blessed by God and become mighty to accomplish His eternal purposes in coming years.

Table of Contents

Acknowledgements ix
Introduction xiii
The River of God-trust xvii

Chapter One: Legacy for Life 19
Chapter Two: Author of Life 43
Chapter Three: Against the Flow 67
Chapter Four: So I Can Serve
    the Lord Better... 97
Chapter Five: Common Sense........................... 129
Chapter Six: Beating the Odds 153
Chapter Seven: Positively Yes! 173

Appendix A: I Accept My Womb 199
Appendix B: Resources..................................... 203
Endnotes 207

Acknowledgements

It has taken over five years to bring this manuscript to the point of publication. During these years my husband and I have seen five more children born into our family (we now have seven), and we have lived on three continents. The Lord has challenged our commitment to let Him be in charge of our lives, and He encouraged me to write this message. My first thanks goes to Him, who saved me and enabled me to complete this task.

Secondly, my husband Jeff has supported, helped, and encouraged me throughout this project and has sacrificed to help it move forward. I love you, Jeff. You are my perfect match. Thank you for helping me persevere. My children – Josef, Joy, John, Hosea, Hosanna, Host, and Christina – thank you for your sacrifices. You are a blessing to me.

Thirdly, many people have given their input into this book. A great big thank you to my sister Naomi and her husband Michel, who custom made illustrations for this book in their studio in Sweden. Thank you, Annette Beasley and Donna Martin, for letting me use your material. Thank you, Rick and Jan Hess, for extending your friendship to us and helping review the chapters. You have been a great blessing to us. Thank you, Pastor Dave Collins, for your input that helped us move forward with the editing. Thank you, Debra Smith, for your excellence in the final reviewing and editing. Your help was invaluable. Thank you to my friend Michelle Harvie and my sister Martha Olsson, for helping me more deeply process the subject through comments and thoughts. Thank you, Cynthia White, for your interest and prayers. There are a number of women, many with large families, who filled in a questionnaire I sent out and added their valuable input. Although only a few are mentioned in this book, they all had a part in it. Thank you for your help and for standing firm in your high calling as mothers. A special thank you to Ed and Shelley Key, who took an interest in the project and helped locate resources for me. A thank you also to Rick and Marilyn Boyer, Elisabeth Elliot, Rick and Jan Hess, Nancy Campbell, and Mary Pride for your interesting and challenging books that strengthened my conviction. Thank you, Winepress Publishing, for helping bring this book into print. I am very grateful for your help and excellence.

Acknowledgements

Finally I want to thank my parents, Lennart and Ingrid Fryxelius, for being a prime example of what it means to give all control of family size to God. Both of you sacrificed for your beliefs, but praise God, you sacrificed yourselves and not your children. Your willingness to break with culture to say *Yes* to God helped Jeff and me dare to trust God for our family size, as well. We love you.

Illustrations by Michel and Naomi Rhodin, Fishpond Entertainment, Sweden

Introduction

I grew up in Sweden as the third oldest in a family of eighteen – dad, mom, ten brothers, and five sisters. Sweden in the seventies was at its peak of submission to the ideal small family size, and we stuck out like a sore thumb. We were recipients of many jokes and crude remarks, but since life was good and we learned that Christians were supposed to be different from the world, we usually took it in stride.

At nineteen years of age I entered the world of missions and lived in south Asia for two years. When I introduced myself and my family background to team members and mission leaders, I realized with a shock that they had adopted the same mentality toward large families as secular Europe! Here we were, serving the Lord…I could walk into a Muslim

Do You Dare Trust God for Your Family Size?

home and they would all bless me for having such a beautiful family at home, while my own leaders viewed children as a hindrance to serving God. Weren't children supposed to be a blessing?

The Lord chose a wonderful husband for me, and we started on our own adventure as parents. We realized quickly that God is much more than just pro-life – He was eager to give us children. When I entered my third pregnancy in three years, we felt an overwhelming need to establish what we believed, for our own sake as well as for those who were concerned for us. Above that, the Lord had started a fire in my soul, a conviction that I needed to write down and then share the answers I found regarding family planning. The chapters ahead are simply the compilation of those answers.

My desire is to see faith and trust in God become the foundation of every Christian life. But for this to happen, there needs to be recognition that culture often works against us to achieve the very opposite. Instead of a clear "In God We Trust," our society would turn our lives into an "In Us We Trust," or the individual icon, "Only in Me I Trust."

This book deals with one specific area of trust for Christians, that of family planning. Elisabeth Elliot wrote, "Nothing in life calls for a deeper humility, a clearer recognition of our own inadequacies and helplessness, and a stronger faith than the gift of parenthood. It is calculated to put us on our faces in the dust."[1] So the question is: Who do we trust? Do we trust ourselves, or do we trust God? Can God be

Introduction

trusted completely for all child planning, for the size of every family, and for the timing of everything?

I believe the Lord wants to confirm to every couple that He can be trusted to plan our families perfectly. Instead of holding on tight to our control, we can give it up to Him. Instead of seeking out cover, we can boldly take a step forward and give ourselves to our faithful God, who works for the good of those who love Him (Rom. 8:28).

If we can trust God in a large life decision like that, I think we can trust Him in every other area as well. Somewhere along that walk of God-trust, we will be found by His exceeding joy. As I pondered the concept of trust, the following story formed in my mind. I pray that it will minister to you the very foundation on which this book has been built–trust in God.

May the Lord God bless you!

The River of God-trust

There was a man, not long ago, who hungered after God. He had already come a long way in life, with plenty of experience and successes. He was well thought of among his friends, a wise investor in any business transaction, and a loyal husband and father. All through his years he kept having the impression that the Lord wanted to do great things through him. In the eyes of his neighbors and friends this was already true, but deep in his subconscious restlessness had taken root. Somehow, he feared he was missing the mark. God must have something else, something greater in mind. And would he ever find out what this thing was?

It could have ended there, had it not been that he cried out to the Lord and was heard. One night, shortly after his personal confession and plea for understanding, he was visited by a dream.

Do You Dare Trust God for Your Family Size?

He found himself on a riverbank, and his eyes were riveted to the water – cascading forth unspeakably clear, and it seemed to him as if singing for joy! In his heart he immediately knew the name of the river: God-trust. A great desire awoke in him to dive into the river and be swept away by the mighty stream, letting it take him anywhere it would lead. But as he made a movement to thrust himself forward, he found – as many find to their dismay in dreams – that he could not move. Unseen fetters were holding his hands and feet in place, and he became aware of a heavy weight on his head, as if he was wearing a helmet of iron. Even over his chest and heart, heaviness was resting and sickened, he understood that he was standing on the bank of Self-trust, and that he long ago had chosen that as his foundation.

As revelation of this mighty, glorious river flooded him, and together with it the knowledge that he unwittingly had chosen the unseemly riverbank, he felt his carefully planned life cave in around him. In despair he cried out, "Have mercy, Lord!"

No sooner had he cried out when he felt the chains fall from him. A strong hand came on his shoulder, as if ready to help him into the river. And the river's song turned into a mighty voice: "Trust in the Lord with all you heart, and lean not on your own understanding…Trust in the Lord with all your heart!"

He plunged into the water's cool embrace.

Legacy for Life

I will stake my life on these three things: that God is alive, His Word is true, and His promises to me will be fulfilled.

A Cultural Pull

Have you realized that we are cultural beings? Has there ever been a person on earth that was not affected by his or her culture? That is what culture is meant to be: a stream of living public opinion, constantly influenced by those who live in it and bravely set the tone, while continually influencing its population toward those same man-made rules, to move a mass of diverse people toward unity. It is a slow tide, seeking constantly to be renewed and changed, yet held in place by the rules set up in the past.

Although all these rules and public opinion come from man to serve his purposes, there are even greater things impacting culture. Strong spiritual forces are at work, quietly introducing new ideas to change whole nations. The changes might seem small enough, but the outcome often takes its citizens by surprise. The Lord is looking for all nations to honor Him, and when they do, He pours out His blessings on them (Deut. 5:10; Ps. 33:12). But when He is forgotten, Satan utilizes culture as a pliable tool to bring in evil in ever-increasing measures to a numbed population. In the various cultures in which I have lived, I have observed this to be true.

It is time to challenge the concepts that the Western culture has welcomed into its bosom during this last century, that of family planning, contraceptives, career thinking, self-fulfillment, and independence. (Hereafter, "Western culture" will mean the generally accepted thoughts that prevail in Europe and

America). The West has accepted this as the norm, and anyone who does not conform will pay the price. To question family planning seems old-fashioned at best and irresponsible at worst. The real problem is that the church has accepted almost the same standard as the world. Although abortion is generally unacceptable in Christian circles, contraceptives are welcomed and even advocated. Culture's voice through 'mature family planning' has become so accepted, in fact, that they are now a normal part of conversation. On almost any Sunday at church I will overhear a man or a woman state, "We have two (or three, or four) children, and we are *done!*" In missionary circles, as well as among pastors and fulltime ministers, the same thoughts pervade.

There is no support for the idea of birth control in God's Word, and I pray that the upcoming chapters will make this abundantly clear. Instead, we need to gain a revelation of what is happening to our culture behind the scenes. Contraceptives were presented as the road to liberty for women, but that is not the real purpose. The purpose is to destroy seed (life), and in particular, a godly seed. Rick Boyer addresses this in his book *Yes, They're All Ours*:

> Throughout the Bible, it was always clear that God loved human life and Satan hated it. God's plan for redemption of the race is the perpetuation of a godly seed. Not surprisingly, Satan's program has consistently been one of trying to destroy the godly seed. Hence the drowning of

Do You Dare Trust God for Your Family Size?

the Hebrew baby boys in the Nile in the day of Pharaoh and the murder by Herod of all the boys under two years old in and around Bethlehem at the time Christ was born. The abortion business today should be recognized as Satanic in origin. When people in hospitals and clinics, trained medical professionals, can look at a trash can full of tiny arms and legs and refer to 'products of conception' rather than murdered babies, the Deceiver has been hard at work.

Boyer further elaborates on the works of Satan:

> He's been busy in the church, as a matter of fact. Attitudes toward childbearing among Christians aren't much closer to the principles of Scripture than among the earth people. We all decry abortion and yet we're so casual toward the issue of human life that we are willing to turn fertility on and off (especially off) like a water faucet. I am not looking to pick a fight with any believer who has honestly searched the Scriptures and come to the conclusion that we have the right to limit the size of our families. To his own Master he stands or falls, and God has the power to change the mind of whichever of us is wrong. It's those who are where I was at the time I got married that I would wrestle with, those who don't see the issue as important enough to warrant prayer and Bible study.[2]

If you are married, you may feel as if your personal territory and choices are being invaded. Please keep in mind as you read that the struggle is not with you. The struggle is with culture and the one who is manipulating it to weaken God's people to the point of complacency. God, on the other hand, has called us to be soldiers for righteousness.

> For our struggle is not against flesh and blood, but against the rulers, against the authorities, against the powers of this dark world and against the spiritual forces of evil in the heavenly realms.
> —Ephesians 6:12

The best thing we can do is to thoroughly search God's Word to determine His purposes for human life, for the church and for our personal lives. If we can come to view life as He sees it and love life as He does, then it will be a joy to join the Creator in the baby business.

THE BASIC COMMAND

> God blessed them and said to them, "Be fruitful and increase in number; fill the earth and subdue it..."
> —Genesis 1:28

"Be fruitful and multiply." This has become a proverbial joke in Christian circles when the talk turns to having children. But the Lord did not intend for this to be a joke. And He could hardly have stated it more clearly.

The first few pages of the Bible acquaint us with a God who creates life with passion! From a vacuum and total silence, life springs forth in a billion ways. As land emerges, a myriad of plants and animals appear on the scene. Going to the zoo is probably the closest we can get in terms of understanding what tremendous joy God had when He created life. The week of creation must have unfolded as an unforgettable saga for the heavenly beings as well—God calling forth all the life forms He had thought out in eternity past, while the angels are gasping for breath, cheering or even standing in awed silence. God loves life! He creates life. He upholds life. He is life.

Immediately after creating plants and animals He gave them the capability to reproduce life according to their own kind. Talk about an abundant Life-giver! Did God realize what an explosion of life would occur? He was obviously not intimidated by the prospect since He decided to establish this as His first and basic command (Gen. 1:11, 22).

On the sixth day the Lord created the first human in His own image, breathing life into him with His own divine breath. Then man also received as his first command to "be fruitful and increase in number" (Gen. 1:28). When the week of creation was completed, all life forms were created by God and revealed His glory, but only man was created in His image. The human race alone was entrusted to portray God's image and character before all generations. Our obedience to this basic command would ensure that the Lord would be well represented on earth by our sheer numbers! Millions of unique images of our God Almighty!

Isn't the Job Already Done?

Those who rely on Genesis to support their views on family size will find themselves in direct conflict with those who embrace the "mission accomplished" theory. This theory states that the biblical command to fill the earth has already been fulfilled; that the earth is full and even has overpopulation problems. Let's give this theory some thought. God's Word says to increase, be fruitful, and fill the earth. In all of Scripture He never indicates that the task will be completed, or that it would be completed before the end of time. In fact, it appears that the task of childbearing will completely end with the final resurrection (Luke 20:27-36). It seems logical to conclude that the second coming of the Lord (as described in Acts 1:11) will bring childbearing to an end (1 Cor. 15:50-52).

I think that if the Lord saw that the task was getting close to being finished, He would intervene by reducing women's fertility level. In Genesis 20:17-18 we read how the Lord closed up every womb in King Abimelech's household for a season. With the ease in which God could do that, I am sure He could and would shut up our wombs if He thought we were overproducing. But since we continue to bear children, we can conclude that the task of increasing is not yet fulfilled. His Word still instructs us to be fruitful, and declares that children are His blessing and gifts to us.

Do You Dare Trust God for Your Family Size?

The theory concerning overpopulation indicates a faulty view of the Lord's character and involvement in our lives. It conjures up a picture of God setting the wheel of baby production in motion and then allowing it to take care of itself and create havoc! This is contradictory to Scripture, which clearly portrays God as lovingly and personally involved in the creation of every human life, even prior to conception. We will see more concerning this in upcoming chapters.

For most couples who regularly use contraceptives, the motive is to stop increasing and become stagnant in their desired family size. It is not to decrease. Yet the nation that follows the same principles and averages about two children per household will decrease, as the death rate exceeds the birth rate.[3]

We read in Proverbs 14:28 that "a large population is a king's glory, but without subjects a prince is ruined." This is already showing itself to be true in Europe, where the low numbers of people has become a serious problem. European countries have had to bring in immigrants to adequately supply their work force. Statistics and studies show that we do not even replenish our own generation with the Western philosophy of family planning. This is not only seriously harming a nation's economy, wealth, stability, and growth[4], but it also operates as a whole to completely contradict God's command to increase in number.

Why would we allow our nation to die out when it is in our power to prevent it? I believe the biggest problem is failing to see and embrace God's purposes for mankind. When we lose sight of His eternal purposes, life tends to narrow down to daily activities and pleasures, and it is easy to forget to plan for future generations. When God is not on the throne of our hearts, we become the greatest contender for it, living in selfish indulgence. That is the state of large parts of the West today. Having and rearing children hinder such a life style.

To address the question of overpopulation, it seems that our view of a full earth is not God's view. He delights in having a multitude of people, and you can be sure that the earth will not see what the Lord would call overpopulation for He counts every head and knows every name. God already controls our fruitfulness by monitoring our life span, He determines the length of time women are able to conceive (teenage to middle age), and the various degree of fruitfulness for each individual couple. He is well aware of every woman's womb, as it is the potential place of creation for another beloved image of Himself.

As of today, the earth is not overpopulated. Rick Hess in *A Full Quiver* writes, "The overpopulation scare is like much of the baggage left over from the sixties - fervently preached by a few, believed by many, but discarded by real leaders and those in the know."[5] He further quotes from the booklet, *How to Understand Humanism* that all peoples on earth could fit into half the city of Jacksonville, Florida, without any person touching another. (I used *Encyclopaedia Britannica 2005* to bring the calculation up to date. I found that we now need three quarters of the city.) The booklet further points out that those who propagate overpopulation assume that a larger population creates a lower living standard, which is not true (as we know from highly populated, yet wealthy Japan, Holland, and the United Kingdom). It is not a high population that brings poverty, but rather national ignorance or misuse of resources, and open rebellion against God's laws.

THE PRIMARY TASK

We have looked at the first command that God gave to mankind, which is to be fruitful. To keep it simple and to help us remember, I've identified it as the basic command. Now I will introduce what I call the primary task. Just like the basic command, it was also revealed before the fall of man:

> The LORD God took the man and put him in the Garden of Eden to work it and take care of it.
> —Genesis 2:15

Adam and his descendants would be God's stewards, governing creation. At that time, God revealed to man that he would need a helper (Gen. 2:18). After Eve was created, the Lord commanded Adam and Eve to be fruitful, to fill the earth and to subdue it (Gen. 1:28). Thus, they were put in charge on earth.

To avoid confusion, let me explain the terms a little further. The basic command and the primary task are commands as well as tasks. I have identified the basic command (reproducing life) as a command to stress the fact that it is an assignment God has given to mankind, and that it is not a suggestion. The primary task is my term to identify that our role on earth is to be stewards of what God has created. Although the care for creation (land and animals) was what God focused sinless Adam's attention to with these words, Scripture points out that since the Fall people are to be our main concern (Matt. 22:37-40). That is the heart of the primary task.

When the resurrected Christ left to return to Heaven, He reminded His followers of the primary task. This time, though, He made sure we understood that the first priority of the task would be concern for our fellow man's final destiny (Matt. 28:18-20). The primary task addresses the greatest desire in the heart of Father God – that each man's lost soul finds its way back to Him. *How can we have this knowledge of God's redemption and hell and yet not share Christ with our friends?* We do not comprehend the awfulness of the coming judgment for the unbeliever, or the pain of love that is hidden in the scars on the hands and feet of Jesus. We need to remember these things daily and to ask the Lord to illumine our hearts with His truth. The truth as He states it, not as we want it to be.

Interestingly enough, the tasks and the commands also work to complete each other! On a personal level we ensure our obedience to carry God's Word to a lost world by raising up godly offspring. We train them by example, lead them to the Lord, and hand them over to His service and in doing so we multiply our service for God's kingdom. One life has multiplied into many and has become a force to be reckoned with. God is glorified, and as Satan's power decreases, the earth is increasingly being governed in God's will – the very thing that the primary task seeks to accomplish!

But let us return to the Genesis account.

THE HELPER

Some women may object to this title; our culture completely rejects it. *The helper.* It seems to indicate by its very name that women were created to fill a subservient role to further an already determined cause. No special assignment for the Helper - the task has already been defined, and she is not holding the main role. He is.

To clear any confusion concerning the role of the helper, let's look at God's plan:

1. He created woman for man to help him complete the two tasks he had received from the Lord: to be fruitful and increase (Gen. 1:28) and to be a steward of God's creation (Gen. 2:15). She was also created to fill his

loneliness and longing for companionship (Gen. 2:18).
2. He created her for himself to raise up godly offspring for His delight and purposes (Mal. 2:15), and to worship Him and create a testimony by her reverent life and good deeds (Rom. 12:1; 1 Tim. 5:9-10, Titus 2:5).
3. He created her for her children to bear the burden of pregnancy and childbirth, and to train, nourish and love them into mature adulthood and usefulness (Mal. 2:15, Titus 2:4-5).

The Lord has given the helper a big chunk of the common task. In my opinion she has the honored task. It was her body that was chosen as the place for God to silently create new life. Even so, the tasks of womanhood have been so ravaged by present day popular opinion, that there is need for further perspective.

God did *not* create man and woman at the same time, and then decide who would get which job. He created man, gave him his tasks, and then later He created woman, and gave her a profile and disposition to fit her purpose. He placed within her certain desires and needs that would find their fulfillment as she carried out her tasks (Gen. 3:16; Prov. 31:25). He made her to be creative and of quiet strength (1 Sam. 25:1-35; Prov. 31:16-18). He imparted to her the disposition of glad surrender and supportive endurance (Song 4:16; 5:9-16; Ruth 1:16-17). He planted within her a desire to be sought out and found worthy, and gave her a need to be wanted and truly needed (Gen. 2:18, 20-24; 3:16; Ruth 2:10-13; Luke 1:38; 46-49).

If man and woman had been created the same, I would understand the feelings of unfairness we so easily nurse today. But He didn't create us the same. He equipped each of us for our own specific tasks, and in working at our tasks we are to find true fulfillment. He also lets us as women know that being a helper is not a bad thing. When Jesus left the earth to return to heaven, He said that He would send a Helper, God the Holy Spirit. *God Himself is willing to take on the role of the lowest servant, as He becomes the Helper of the helper (woman)!* The Lord is both almighty and humble. We need not be ashamed to imitate Him in service. The humble servant will be exalted in due time (Matt. 11:29; Luke 14:11).

In today's world we have created cheap substitutions, as it offers women fame, success, and moments of carefree indulgence. But the woman who has come to know God doesn't trade. God offers her something better—fulfillment—and what one faithful wife and mother described to me as "a deep, inexpressible joy."

By accepting the fact that God made man and woman different and for different tasks, the battle for the modern woman ends. Our culture tells us that man and woman are in essence the same, and that a woman's true fulfillment is found when she wrestles her way to center stage and takes charge of the main role, which belongs to the man. But this present-day theory is ignoring well known facts about women's physical design and deeply engraved programming for worship, wifehood and motherhood.[6] Listening to women around me, I hear constant regrets of having spent too much time in the work force and too little time at home with husband and children. I haven't heard even one mother regret the opposite! In future chapters, we will explore further how our God-given tasks can truly lead us to complete fulfillment and joy. But we need to return to Genesis for one more look.

THE FALL AND THE MYTH

Eve became Adam's perfect match, filling his void for companionship and giving him two extra hands to accomplish his tasks. Not only did they experience productive teamwork, they also had fulfillment. They had relationship with God, they had each other, and they were eager to begin their service! The conditions and surroundings were ideal.

Then came the fall only a short time after they had come together and began disrupting how things were supposed to work. Satan has a hard time tolerating anything divine or that which reminds him of who is in charge. Of all God's creation, he hated Adam and Eve the most for they displayed God's image morning, noon and night! At this point God had already hurled Satan out of heaven for his rebellion and lust for ultimate power. Having been thrown down to earth, Satan then saw God entrusting leadership on earth to beings who were created later in time and seemingly "lower" than himself! I am sure he realized in the Garden that it would just get worse as Adam and Eve began to have children, and they also shined! Mankind was for him not only an object of hatred because of who they reminded him of; they were also competition. It would be best to do something about the matter before any offspring appeared.

He decided the thing to do was to test these humans' trust in God with a simple question of authority. Should God be in charge of everything, or could Adam and Eve decide a few things for themselves? You know, grow up and understand how things should run, instead of this childish dependence on God all the time? (Gen. 3:1-4)

Eve fell flat for that one and so did Adam after only a little persuasion. Sin, in the form of simple disobedience to God's rule, unleashed the curse that would haunt every baby to be born – inherited sinful nature, and spiritual lethargy taking the place of pulsating life brought by fellowship with God. They also found that their sin created burdensome work by hardening the ground and spurred on severe pain in childbearing. Quite a package deal.

Have you heard the myth, that it was not the eating of the fruit that was the original sin, but that it was *sex* that sent the human race spinning? If that was true, then the marriage bed, that God meant for couples to enjoy and delight in, became a shameful, secret thing. With such a fundamental misconception, couples feel they are carrying on with lustful indulgence rather than a joyful union that the Bible describes as "becoming one flesh" or "to know" each other. Sex within marriage is an intimate gift from God, designed to be so exciting and good that husband and wife can enjoy their oneness for a lifetime. The task of reproduction becomes a joy instead of a tedious chore. In fact, for us who are believers, we know that sex within marriage is a holy experience; God works there, not only to bring about oneness, but to create new living beings that He proclaims holy as well (1 Cor. 7:14). Satan is the one who doesn't want couples to enjoy their married life or to see their offspring as a blessing.

My mother wrote in a testimonial that sex actually works as a contraceptive against sin! A contraceptive works as a shield to protect us from something. In 1 Corinthians 7:5 Paul tells us that sex within marriage operates as a shield against adultery. It is important to know what we should shield ourselves from, for it is not the fruit of married life (children), but rather from sin itself.

Dependency on God or Not

Let's look for a moment at the temptation Satan offered Adam and Eve. He offered independence from the will of God and knowledge of good and evil. Their decision to take the offer impacts the whole area of family planning to this day.

Dependency is not a popular word nowadays. Instead, we hear an underlying theme that communicates, "Be your own person," "Choose your own way," "Be strong in yourself," and so forth. Born-again Christians who accept that they need God begin this new path by breaking with the trends of culture. They confess their dependency on the Lord in more and more areas of their lives as the Spirit awakens them to the truth. This is not to say that we become incapable of mature participation in society; rather, God molds us into the true person He planned for us to become. While culture calls all citizens to 'grow up' and learn to think independently (which usually means being molded to the pattern of society), God calls for us to become like little children in childlike dependence on Him and to learn obedience as beloved sons and daughters. Jesus Himself is our forerunner, as the apostle John reminds us,

> ...as the Father has sent Me, I am sending you.
> —John 20:21

He humbled Himself and served the Father in full submission. Satan insinuates that we obey God out of fear of punishment or weak character, while Jesus showed that true submission and chosen dependency flows from our love and the security of our position as God's children. He said,

> ...the prince of this world is coming. He has no hold on me, but the world must learn that I love

the Father and that I do exactly what my Father has commanded me.
—John 14:30-31

The Apostle John further reminds us,

This is love for God: to obey His commands. And His commands are not burdensome, for everyone born of God overcomes the world.
—1 John 5:3-4

This scripture tells us that His commands are not burdensome, yet if you listen to opinions around you it will tell you the opposite. Modern culture finds God's commands burdensome, because it cannot fit God's law into its agenda. Just as the flesh and the Spirit are in constant opposition because of their conflicting desires (Gal. 5:16-18), so also can a selfish culture not agree to adhere to divine directives. Instead, it makes it increasingly difficult for anyone to obey God's commands without heavy attention and mockery. The burden is not from God, but rather from our own godless culture.

Concerning this topic, independency from God can be found in statements such as these:

- "When I first became a Christian, I was so dependent on God. But I am growing up and don't need Him as much anymore." (Meaning: Dependency in God is a thing we should grow away from.)

- "One shouldn't have more children than one can care for." (Meaning: More than I can handle without God's help.)
- "God wants me to be happy, and so having kids is for those who enjoy kids or feel called." (Meaning: Obedience is not so important to God, as long as I feel good about things.)
- "We are God's co-workers, so He lets us choose how many children we would like to have." (Meaning: What God meant with being fruitful was merely a suggestion and a general blessing, not a command.)

These are thoughts of man and they act as smoke screens to cover our unwillingness to walk according to God's plan for our lives.

Now, let us move from our observations of Genesis and take a look at what happens at the cross.

A Picture of Heaven

During the sleep of the second Adam (Jesus' death on the cross) God started forming a woman for Him (the church). Although the cross came "late in time," it was the prototype from which God formed the first marriage, that of Adam and Eve. Every believer is part of this heavenly woman (the church, the bride of Christ), who will not be fully revealed until the last times when the full score of believers have been reached. This is the purpose of God for us from before we were even conceived, that we would belong to this Man, Jesus.

At the time we first believed, God's Spirit entered our lives and gave us a yearning to know our Lord, the bridegroom. We discovered that our new purpose in life was to please Him, and prepare ourselves to meet Him. As we continue in our pursuit of godliness, we find that we are learning to listen to His written directions and inner leading, and that it's becoming easier and easier to yield our wills to His purposes. We have entered an unseen reality, and we live to please the one we have come to love and know intimately and who knows us completely.

God created marriage to portray this union with Himself. In Ephesians 5:22-33 we see how we are to function. For those of us who were created as women, we show by our submission to our husbands how much we love Jesus and our willingness to obey Him. Husbands portray the Lord as they protect and provide for their wives and children (both physically and spiritually), and they have to lay down their lives in many ways. They are also part of the bride (the church), and so they, too, humble themselves and serve the Lord in a complete equality and togetherness with their wives. For there is no difference between man and woman in their standing before Him (Gal. 3:28); there is only a difference in earthly function and degree of responsibility.

Not only in our unity as married couples do we portray God, but also through our fruitfulness. True love always produces fruit. Jesus died to raise up the church and it is He who, with the aid of His bride, brings forth disciples from every nation. He is daily adding children to the household of God (those who are being saved), and we can see no sign of Him becoming tired of His work! Even though we, as married couples, are a small scale picture of this heavenly drama, our unwillingness to be fruitful causes us to be a very poor picture of this. For the Lord works intently on His task of bringing His children in, not wanting anyone to perish. And for every new birth, there is great rejoicing among the angels (Luke 15:7). They, too, are deeply interested in the baby business. They understand that it is how the Lord receives both glory and satisfaction.

Purposed for Fruitfulness

It is interesting to compare the first command of God (to be fruitful) with the last command of Jesus (to go and make disciples), and see that they both tell us to be agents for bringing forth new life: first in the natural, and then in the spiritual. That is not an accident. Rather, it is the Lord wanting to emphasize what is important to Him; first life, and then having that life connected to the mainstream – God Himself. Jesus stated:

> The thief comes only to steal and kill and destroy; I have come that they may have life and have it to the full.
> —John 10:10

It is love that moves us to action. We are commanded to love, and to bear fruit. We are not surprised to find that the whole Bible finds its fulfillment in simply loving Him and others.

> Jesus replied, "Love the Lord your God with all your heart and with all your soul and with all your mind. This is the first and greatest commandment. And the second is like it: Love your neighbor as yourself. All the law and the Prophets hang on these two commandments."
> —Matthew 22:37-40

In the intimate love relationship of man and wife, children are conceived. And in the passionate love for our Savior, we reach out to our fellow man and see him born again. So simple; yet culture has made it so complex.

As we continue our journey toward understanding God's intentions for human life, keep in mind the story of the man who fell headlong into the stream of God-trust (see Introduction). While we study God's Word and weigh it against modern reasoning, it will help make it clear that welcoming children into our families has become a matter of faith for our time, a matter of trusting the Lord and daring to take the plunge.

Chapter Two

Author of Life

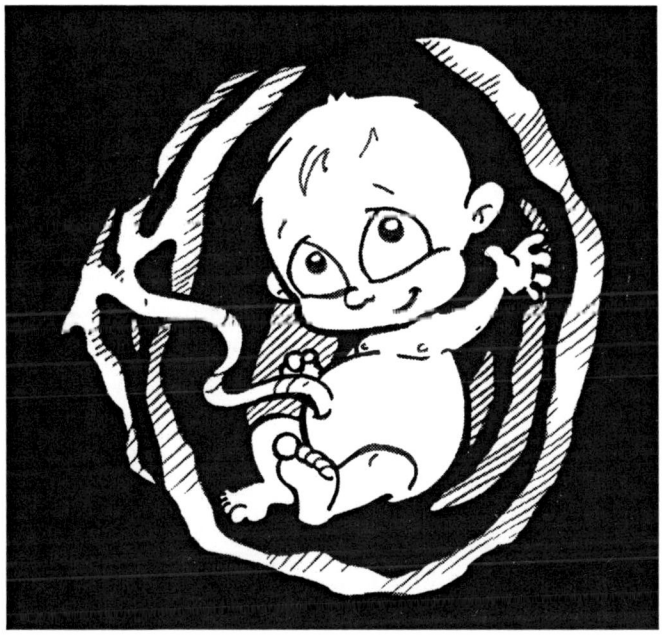

For You created my inmost being; You knit me together in my mother's womb. I praise You because I am fearfully and wonderfully made; Your works are wonderful, I know that full well… All the days ordained for me were written in Your book before one of them came to be.

—Psalm 139:13-14, 16

With License to Choose

I have found in both Europe and America, that the whole topic of conception and contraception has been sweetly blanketed by believers in the name of tolerance which states, "Your way is right for you, and I have by the law of public opinion no right to suggest you should do differently." Many agree that in the very personal matter of family planning, God has handed us our *license to choose* whether or not we want children, when we want them, and how many we should have. It seems so reasonable. We are God's co-workers and are created in His image with clear thinking capabilities and ability to evaluate our family situations. We can make good choices to usher us into a desirable future and avoid things we feel could potentially be too much. Many people seem to feel strongly that with too many children around, they would not have a chance to become all God wants them to be or to do all He has for them to do.

Forget for a moment about being tolerant, and let us ask what God thinks. First, did He hand us this license to choose, or is it man-made? As the Creator, does He mind if we personally decide our family size? Does it bother Him if we use contraceptives, as long as we have some good reasons for it? Even though technology has provided us with the means to prevent conception, should we use them? Or does His title, Creator, mean *author of life - all rights reserved*?

WE BELONG TO GOD!

First, let's ask this: Does God have a claim on our lives? Whether He claims His right or not, He is our creator. He made us, and by being our maker, He owns us. Although He has given us the ability to choose whom we will serve - God or the evil one - it is clear that this is a temporary state and that in the end, every knee will bow to Him (Phil. 2:9-11). Whether we admit it or not, we are His idea, and with His almighty power He could do whatever He wanted to with us. Jeremiah wrote:

> I know, O LORD, that a man's life is not his own;
> it is not for man to direct his steps.
> —Jeremiah 10:23

Though our hearts might rebel against the idea of God's sovereignty over our lives, we need to remember that He is not a harsh God. He works gently with us – not capriciously, but lovingly – to achieve goals that are far beyond our understanding. He made us ultimately for His own delight and pleasure, so that He could know us, love and care for us, and reveal His glory through us (Gen. 1:26, Zeph. 3:17; Isa. 43:7; Eph. 1:4-6). We were not made for ourselves! We were not made to think only of our own situation, scrambling to make sense of life and make the best of it. The Creator made us for Himself and desires for us to realize this and step into the place of honor He has reserved for each one of us. We are created in His image, purposed for fellowship through Jesus, and satisfied through fruitful service. You have heard it before – God loves you and has a wonderful plan for your life. It is true.

God made everything well, but He stamped mankind as His own image. On every one of us is His seal of approval. *This one is mine. I made you. I am proud of the work I have done. I love you.* The very fact that we look like God (not only outwardly, but in mind and soul as well), shows that we belong to Him in a unique way. For fallen man, the truth of God's ownership might be a hard fact, but for everyone who trusts in Him it brings great comfort and purpose to life.

HOLD YOUR BREATH!

Actually, you don't have to. He is holding it for you. If being the Creator would not be claim enough on our lives, this would be. Colossians 1:16-17 states:

> For by Him [Christ] all things were created: things in heaven and on earth, visible and invisible, whether thrones or powers or rulers or authorities; all things were created by Him and for Him. He is before all things, and in Him all things hold together.

About animals, in Psalms 104:29 states:

> ...when You take away their breath, they die and return to the dust.

In Genesis we see Adam receive the breath of life through God's own breath (Gen. 2:7). Isaiah 38:1-8 recounts that God listened to a dying king's plea and added fifteen years of guaranteed breath to his life! Just as easily, He took the breath from Ananias and Sapphira because of their deception. They dropped dead on the spot (Acts 5:1-11). We are not able to even breathe without God!

Interestingly enough, we find that Jesus, as the incarnate Son, was still holding His own breath while on earth. Death could not touch Him until He was ready to hand Himself over (John 10:17-18; Luke 23:46). It is good for us to remember who is the Master of our very breath and heartbeat. It adds a healthy respect for life, and also destroys the fear of death, for nothing can touch your life unless allowed by God Himself.

A Time and a Season

> There is a time for everything, and a season for every activity under heaven: a time to be born and a time to die...
> —Ecclesiastes 3:1-2

Scripture makes it clear that God works through times and seasons. God Himself stands outside of time, living in eternity. You can see it by the name I Am (Exodus 3:14), that He gave Himself. This *I Am* is a curious title without a specific time reference in Hebrew. It can mean I Was, or I Am, or I Will Be (see also Rev. 1:8). Even though we as humans move along the time line He has established, God Himself is not limited to it. This is seen in the sacrifice of Christ. Even though He was born and crucified at the exact moment in time God assigned (Gal. 4:4, John 17:1), He was also offering Himself outside of time, in heaven, so that His sacrifice would be sufficient for all time and for all people (1 Peter 1:20).

It seems that every plan and purpose of God takes place in eternity (Eccl. 3:1, 11, 14), and He assigns its realization on earth with a fixed point in time. Jesus was so attuned to the necessary timing and fulfillment of His tasks, that He several times had to remind His disciples of His need to wait for the Father's timing (John 2:4; Matt. 26:18; Mark 14:41; John 12:23). Naturally, we are not always aware of what God's timing is for things to happen. Jesus' brothers thought any time was good for Him to reveal His miracles or be acknowledged by the crowds, but Jesus replied:

> The right time for me has not yet come; for you any time is right. The world cannot hate you, but it hates me because I testify that what it does is evil. You go to the Feast. I am not yet going to this Feast, because for me the right time has not yet come.
> —John 7:6-8

This is the one we are urged to imitate, Jesus (1 John 2:6). In the midst of the noise and suggestions from His brothers, His spirit is in tune with the Father and He knows that the timing is wrong. For that seemingly small reason, He stays faithfully behind while the others take off. Timing. As He moved, so should we move with God, without haste or delay.

Do I dare tell you that contraceptives are far from the thought of God's timing? It was invented for the very reason of getting around it. It is stating bluntly, "My way, in my time." And as we let our desires and demands speak, we drown the quiet guidance of the Spirit, and miss the right time. Of course, God always has backup plans, redeeming our shortcomings and showering us with His grace. But it is His goal that we grow up and become like His Son.

I am beginning to recognize, as the above quote from Ecclesiastes shows, that there truly are God-ordained times and seasons for everything. It is usually easier to realize that great historic events need a specific time for their fulfillment than that God truly guides us through every season of our lives. As I recognize the season I am in, and am faithful to respond accordingly to the Lord, then I am put on the road to spiritual maturity. For example, I have now as a married woman entered the season of childbearing, and am learning how to be a godly wife and mother. It is so practical and such a long season (that actually spans many seasons in other areas of my life), that it is hard to comprehend how it can be significant in my service to God. Sometimes it seems all the motherly duties actually hinder other service. It helps me to view this season of my life from my Savior's point of view:

> He tends His flock like a Shepherd; He gathers the lambs in His arms and carries them close to His heart; He gently leads those that have young.
> —Isaiah 40:11

It is definitely not the picture of a hurried life style or that anything is being accomplished except the perfect well-being of mother and young. I am learning that the Lord is accomplishing His purposes for me as the days go by and I tend to my little ones. He has designed this season to be slow and steady, not fast and burning. And that is good, for motherhood takes all I have!

I believe one of Satan's tricks to discourage us is to make us believe that the season we are in will go on forever. A simple acknowledging of God-ordained seasons in our lives with a knowing that they will pass, will keep discouragement away from us and help us endure until we see change.

Thoroughly Planned

Keeping in mind that God created us, stamped us as His own personal belongings and to this day still upholds our breath, let us now take a look at how well-planned our lives are before our birth – from before Creation, to conception, and up to the time of delivery.

God knew that He would make you before He even created the world.

> For He chose us in Him before the creation of the
> world to be holy and blameless in His sight.
> —Ephesians 1:4

To be able to choose us, He must have seen us. When He made humans, it was not as an afterthought to His magnificent work on Creation, to top it off. We were in His mind and already sealed in Him before He even began to create!

God knew everything about you before you were conceived, and He planned your life then. The Lord said to Jeremiah,

> Before I formed you in the womb I knew you,
> before you were born I set you apart; I appointed
> you as a prophet to the nations.
> —Jeremiah 1:5

Do you think Jeremiah was a special case because He had a prophetic ministry waiting for him? No. God has ministries waiting for all of us, and they will be distributed by the Holy Spirit (1 Cor. 12:4-6, 12). We are all created to show forth His glory; that is why we are all God's special ones! Although not all of us hear a prophetic utterance of what we will be doing in our lives, there is no denying that every single human will affect many, and possibly thousands of lives during his or her lifetime. A person given to the Lord will find that his life constantly influences the people around him for good. From our mother's womb we were created to make history!

Do You Dare Trust God for Your Family Size?

God took His time to form you and love you while you were in the womb. Unseen by all others, He had His nine months of exclusive work on you, delighting in making you just right, desirable in His sight.

> For You created my inmost being; You knit me together in my mother's womb. I praise You, because I am fearfully and wonderfully made; Your works are wonderful, I know that full well. My frame was not hidden from You when I was made in the secret place. When I was woven together in the depths of the earth, Your eyes saw my unformed body. All the days ordained for me were written in Your book before one of them came to be.
> —Psalm 139:13-16

> Your hands made and formed me...
> —Psalm 119:73

God did more than merely outline the main events of your life. Take a look at Psalms and Ephesians:

> Many, O LORD my God, are the wonders You have done. The things You planned for us no one can recount to You; were I to speak and tell of them, they would be too numerous to count.
> —Psalm 40:5

> For we are God's workmanship, created in Christ Jesus to do good works, which God prepared in advance for us to do.
> —Ephesians 2:10

It is so comforting to know there is a purpose for our lives. There are no qualifications needed to be productive in God's eyes – any upbringing, education, intellect, skill or appearance will do, as long as there is a fellowship between us and the Lord. We all serve a purpose and by simply walking in our own personally defined God-purpose we bring Him the greatest joy and satisfaction and are ourselves fulfilled.

A God Who is Very Present

This same God, who seals us and plans our lives, is also personally involved in the progress to see his new image bearer come to conception, maturation and birth. Is there evidence that God is near at conception? There is. Psalm 104:24, 30 teaches us the following:

> How many are Your works, O LORD! In wisdom You made them all; the earth is full of Your creatures...When You send Your Spirit, they are created, and You renew the face of the earth.

These verses speak of animals who mean less to the Lord than human life (Matt. 6:26), yet He cares for them. Even with them, the Lord sends His own Spirit to oversee and care for the conception process. Does He do any less for us? No, the Bible clearly indicates that it is He who made us. It is not our parents who have the responsibility for how their children turn out (i.e. appearance, capabilities and personality); though they were partakers in creating life, the Lord lays the responsibility on Himself.

> You turn things upside down, as if the potter were thought to be like the clay! Shall what is formed say to Him who formed it, 'He did not make me'? Can the pot say of the potter, 'He knows nothing'?
> —Isaiah 29:16

The patriarch Jacob even became angry with his wife Rachel because she was ignorant of who gave conception.

> When Rachel saw that she was not bearing Jacob any children, she became jealous of her sister. So she said to Jacob, "Give me children, or I'll die!" Jacob became angry with her and said, "Am I in the place of God, Who has kept you from having children?"
> —Gen 30:1-2

These Scriptures tell us that God is present at conception and is the initiator of it. This will become even clearer as we look at the barren and fertile womb.

Just as God is present at conception, He is also the initiator of the moment of birth. In Psalm 71:6 it states,

> ...You brought me forth from my mother's womb.

The same is found in Psalm 22:9-10 and Job 10:18. These verses bring special encouragement to me when I am in the delivery room. There are a thousand things that potentially could go wrong during a normal delivery, yet percentage-wise very little does. I am convinced it is because God is very present and personally involved in bringing His new little creations into sight. Like the artist, He would not want to miss the uncovering of His own work. And it is in the delivery room that doctors, nurses, parents and other attendees stand in reverent awe over the miracle of birth and a beautiful new arrival, another image-bearer. Even nonreligious people testify there to the presence of God.

As we have been looking at these Bible passages, I again want to make this point clear; although I may be the honored woman of a pregnancy, I am not the maker of the baby – nor is my husband. I am the mother (nurturer) of this new life – the Lord uses my body to nourish the baby, but He is the Maker. Once He has finished the work in the womb, He brings out a new image-bearer (His baby!) and gives me and my husband full trust in raising him or her to maturity. This is not just another theological conclusion; it should revolutionize how we view childbearing and child rearing. If they are all the Lord's, then it is easy to accept the responsibility to receive them into our wombs, and to train them without carrying our personal ambitions for them. There will be freedom to love and train, anticipating only what the Lord will accomplish through them.

Do You Dare Trust God for Your Family Size?

A Gift, a Blessing, and a Reward

When I was growing up, we had a neighbor lady from a different country who sometimes stopped to visit with my mother. She was nice but also a little odd. One Christmas she decided to give some of us little gifts. My oldest brother received a ketchup bottle. Another brother received a soap bar. And I received a can of powdered drink which I did not open for months because it looked so strange. The gifts were well intended but were ill-matched. God's gifts to us are not like that. Looking at God's character and what the Bible reveals to us about Him, we come to these conclusions:

1. God gives gifts to give joy to the receiver and to bless him.
2. God plans His gifts carefully and they are intended to have enduring positive effects on us.
3. God's gifts are very personal and specially made by Him for you. No gift is mass produced.
4. The Giver knows you intimately and understands your character and needs and matches His gift accordingly.
5. Every gift is good and perfect (James 1:17).

Likewise, God's blessings are meant for our good and in them we can perceive what He is like. A blessing is somewhat different from what most of us would think it is. The word *blessing* in Hebrew (barak) means, among other things, to kneel. God makes something happen or gives us something that causes us to stretch spiritually and helps us to come to a place of brokenness (kneeling) before Him. A blessing is something that brings us to the Lord. As we submit to the challenge which He brings, He can pour out on us His divine favor - which we usually think of as the real blessing.

This kind of blessing (the kneeling) definitely occurs with having children since they reduce our freedom to indulge ourselves and keep us serving. Mary Pride writes, "What 'freedom' do babies cost us? Do they interfere with our freedom to love and serve God? No; they interfere with our freedom to indulge 'the lustful desires of sinful human nature', as Peter puts it, ranging from common childish selfishness to full-fledged adult depravity."[7]

God's blessing is the best we can ever wish for ourselves or for someone we love. God calls children gifts and a blessing from Him. Satan is trying his hardest to make us forget this. While it is easier to pray for spiritual blessings and extraordinary gifts, I pray God will make us desire the gift and blessing of having children in our homes.

Scripture also states that children are a reward from God (Psalm 127:3). It is odd to think that a divine reward should be despised by men, but culture has managed to do just that. What God calls a reward man calls a burden. A very fruitful womb (i.e. a woman who has had ten children in eleven years) is seen as a curse and the woman's life is viewed as a disaster! Compare this to the response of Leah, despite her marital problems:

> When the LORD saw that Leah was not loved, he opened her womb, but Rachel was barren. Leah became pregnant and gave birth to a son. She named him Reuben, for she said, "It is because the LORD has seen my misery"...Second son, "Because the LORD heard that I am not loved." Third son, "Now at last my husband will become attached to me..." And fourth son, "This time I will praise the LORD."
> —Genesis 29:31-35

She saw that despite her misery, the Lord was rewarding her with children and they helped her to see that she was not rejected by God.

The word *reward* implies that something has been earned. It may be earned favor, an attitude of a willing heart, faithfulness to carry out the Lord's business, or a variety of other things. You should know that when the Lord grants you and your spouse conception, He is sending you a divine reward. That, in itself, is enough to help us lift our heads with new confidence. Proverbs 13:21 states that prosperity is the reward of the righteous. But there is more!

Children themselves are a reward. Just as God is our ultimate *great reward* (Gen. 15:1), children as God's image-bearers are *small great rewards*. They are carriers forever of God-breathed life and they will see eternity. Having a child is to have another piece of eternity close to you and in your care. The satisfaction of seeing your children grow, live, make good choices, and become mature adults is, for most parents, a satisfaction beyond comparison. In chapter seven we will see how children will also *bring* a reward for all who have raised them. They are a sure way for us to produce fruit for God!

A Holy Place

For us as believers we know that our bodies, including the womb, have been made holy because of the indwelling of the Holy Spirit and the sanctification that follows. In 1 Corinthians 3:16-17 we find,

> Don't you know that you yourselves are God's temple and that God's Spirit lives in you? If anyone destroys God's temple, God will destroy him; for God's temple is sacred, and you are that temple.

Furthermore, 1 Corinthians 6:19-20 says:

> Do you not know that your body is a temple of the Holy Spirit, who is in you, whom you have received from God? You are not your own; you were bought at a price. Therefore honor God with your body.

In everything we do, we are to honor God in our conduct and with our bodies. In Romans 12:1 we are urged to go even further and make it a commitment of self-surrender:

> Therefore, I urge you, brothers, in view of God's mercy, to offer your bodies as living sacrifices, holy and pleasing to God - this is your spiritual act of worship.

For the woman, this includes a surrender of the womb. In fact, the word *woman* that Adam gave to Eve means *man with a womb*.[8] The womb is the major thing that defines womanhood. By surrendering the womb to serve the Lord, couples open up the door for God to truly work out His plans for them *and* for their children. All throughout the Bible women were counted as blessed by the Lord if they were fruitful in childbearing. The feminist movement has wanted to change this, and instead, portray a fruitful womb as a curse of overproduction and in need of fast medical attention.[9] Remarkably, they have not been able to reverse barrenness into a blessing. It continues to be a heartache to those who experience it.

THE BARREN WOMB

There has been a stigma of shame attached to the barren couple. In many ways, the church has played a part in placing the shame on the couple by quoting Bible passages that may or may not apply to their situation which creates more pain and confusion than help. The serious study of God's Word offers great encouragement and provides solutions.

It shows that barrenness can come from several different sources:

1. Not *accepting fertility as a blessing.* This might be a very normal cause for barrenness in our age, although it is little understood. When God pronounces His work to be good (i.e. the womb) and man pronounces it to be evil, there is a curse of rebellion coming into play (Isa. 5:20; Mal. 2:2). Agreeing with a culture that does not value fertility can create such a curse. A woman I know learned from her mother to call her monthly bleeding the curse. She continued to have irregular periods for many years until she realized that she was cursing what God had meant to be a blessing. After she prayed and repented, her monthly cycle became more regular.

   If, in your past, you know you have been angry about being a woman and have cursed God (either in your heart or aloud) for your period, womb, breasts, or have been involved in immoral living, vowed never to have children, etc., this may be a cause for current unfruitfulness. (The same may be true for the man who has despised the thought of fatherhood or was involved in immorality and in so doing placed himself under a curse.) It can also be helpful to do a family history check, to see if anyone close to you has made very strong statements of hate toward reproduction. Simple repentance and renouncing of those acts, and asking God to bless will be enough to lift the curse (Gen. 49:22-26; Ex. 34:6-7; 1 John 1:9).

> Then Abraham prayed to God, and God healed Abimelech, his wife and his slave girls so they could have children again, for the LORD had closed up every womb in Abimelech's household because of Abraham's wife Sarah.
> —Genesis 20:17-18

2. *The barren womb can be a fertile ground for miracles.* Often the Lord chooses to let us wait for His blessing for reasons of His own. Although He had promised to make Abraham's descendants as numerous as the stars, all three patriarchs had to wait on God while their wives bore the sorrow of barrenness. Sarah had to wait the longest, and her faith was sorely tested. But to her a son would mean more than just release from shame. It was a promise from God, and confirmed God to be trustworthy even in impossible situations.

> Then the LORD said to Abraham, "Why did Sarah laugh and say, 'Will I really have a child, now that I am old?' Is anything too hard for the LORD?"
> —Genesis 18:13-14, 21:1-2

Isaac became her joy and comfort. Isaac and Rebekah faced barrenness and it was not lifted until Isaac interceded on behalf of his wife. Then the Lord granted them twins who became two nations (Gen. 25:21-23). Jacob had to rebuke his wife Rachel for her ignorance of where babies came from, and even then she decided to walk in the natural by taking matters into her own hands and use her maidservant as a surrogate womb. It was not until many years later that the Lord showed her pity in her frantic pursuit for fruitfulness (Gen. 30).

Consider Hannah, the barren wife of Elkanah (1 Sam. 1-2). The wait for a son made her desperate enough to prepare her for the sacrifice ahead. She promised the Lord her son, if only she could bear him. That put Samuel in the place he needed to be for God's purposes for the whole nation of Israel.

I believe there are many couples who desperately seek the Lord for a child and yet they will have to wait on Him. I have heard many testimonies of barrenness completely removed without any medical input by prayer and trust in Almighty God. Continue to ask Him. The wait may be long, but when the answer arrives, be prepared to train your child and to see your son or daughter grow up to fulfill a very specific role in God's Kingdom!

3. *God has other plans.* Barrenness might also be a *no* in the physical for a higher *yes* in the spiritual. Whether you carry a child in the womb or not, the function of family is still there. A woman will always have God's call to nurture, whether it be through a ministry (Sunday school, missions, neighborhood), adoption, or as a *fisherman* - becoming a spiritual mother to many. The Lord does promise that the barren woman will see more children than the one who has her own (Isaiah 54:1). She then becomes fruitful beyond the natural! The same applies for the woman or man who is called to be single. In the kingdom realm they are still placed in a family (Psalm 68:6), and then He makes them able to produce life through their assigned service. To bear sons and daughters is for EVERYONE - man and woman, single or married. We are all image-bearers of Father God from whom all families derive their name (Ephesians 3:14-15).

A Matter of Choice

We are back to the question of the license to choose. After studying the Scriptures, we have found that God, by His very nature and desire, is completely pro-life. He plans life, He creates life and He imparts the ability for fruitfulness to all living things. He chooses life.

When God allowed the fall and for man to choose his own way, He knew that we, with our advanced capabilities and skills as His image-bearers, would be able to create and devise many things which could be for either good or harm. In all our advancements, He allows us to choose between good and evil. That does not mean He approves. There are things that are evil in His sight, but He waits with judgment.

> These things you have done and I kept silent;
> you thought I was altogether like you...
> —Psalm 50:21

If God chooses life, we need to choose life with Him. We can do nothing less if we want to stand with Him. If we do not choose life, we do choose death, whether actively destroying it (abortion) or more passively preventing it (contraceptives). There is no neutral ground between the Kingdom and the world. That is why Jesus matter-of-factly stated that we would be hated for His sake (John 15:18-20).

Joshua felt keenly the battle for wills as he stated to the people of Israel their choice:

> Now fear the LORD and serve Him with all faithfulness. Throw away the gods your forefathers worshipped..., and serve the LORD. But if serving the LORD seems undesirable to you, then

Do You Dare Trust God for Your Family Size?

choose for yourselves this day whom you will serve, whether the gods your forefathers served beyond the River, or the gods of the Ammorites, in whose land you are living. But as for me and my household, we will serve the LORD.
—Joshua 24:14-15

Against the Flow

Like arrows in the hands of a warrior are sons born in one's youth. Blessed is the man whose quiver is full of them. They will not be put to shame when they contend with their enemies in the gate.

—Psalm 127:4-5

In the previous chapters we looked at God's perspective and involvement in human life. We found that He is very involved indeed. Now it is time to examine ourselves – modern man. What is our perspective? What do we think about being fruitful? When we attempt to control our fertility, what are our underlying motives and attitudes? We also need to take a second look into the Creator's master plan for families and rediscover a forgotten tool of war.

Abortion

Let us first take a look at abortion which is an extreme method of human control. Or shall we call it out of control? Here the unfathomable is happening in civilized society—innocent lives being ravaged while the masses are lured into slumber. Satan does not need to mask his hate toward God's image-bearers, but devours his plunder like a roaring lion (1 Peter 5:8). Anyone who researches the methods used to abort a baby will be chilled to the bone. Abortion is a flaunted evil and the church recognizes that. We are shocked to discover, however, that even among evangelical Christians the abortion rates are high – up to 234,000 abortions in a given year. This is reported by Lois Cunningham of the Center for Bioethical Reform, a pro-life research and development organization. The reason stated is social pressure from within the church. "Christians abort because they are Christians," says Molly, a crisis pregnancy counselor. "It is easier to hide the abortion than the pregnancy. It's the mentality that asks, 'Who would you rather face, Jesus as a judge or your Christian peers?"[10] Again, we see the cultural influence to be stronger than the fear of the Lord. It is sad that the church often encourages outward appearances of righteousness, rather than confession and repentance of sin. Commonly, the shame is also misplaced and laid on the baby rather than on the sin of immoral living. But there is never a need to repent of a baby! Children are always a gift and a blessing. The real need is for the parents of the child to realize that they have stepped out of God-given boundaries and they need to repent of their sin and restore their fellowship with the Lord.

The Lord Jesus commissioned His church to be salt and light to the world through word, deed and attitude (Matt. 5:13-16). The abortion issue is just the tip of the iceberg - it is rightly protested and decried. But the task goes much deeper, into the heart attitude of a world that is increasingly hostile toward children. Have you awakened to the shocking reality that we as a people do not love children anymore? There is still an openness and desire by couples planning to have a baby. But is there space in our hearts for any child God would bring into our path? The church has unwittingly fallen under the influence of this anti-child attitude. It is easy to protest the obvious flaunted sin of abortion; it is another thing to deal with the silent hardening of hearts within the church. As we study the motives for contraceptives and the model for a healthy church community, we will see this more clearly and find some solutions.

Do You Dare Trust God for Your Family Size?

I want to mention a few very common human excuses for abortion that permeates our society and invades our thinking if we are not careful. Donna Martin, a friend of mine, wrote these answers for a radio talk show, and she allowed me to share them with you. Enjoy her personality and sharp edge!

Let's talk. Some of the arguments [for abortion]:

"It's my body." It is most definitely not just your body. That baby has a different set of fingerprints, formed, or about to be, a different brainwave pattern, possibly even a different blood type. You may be the unhappy hostess to an unplanned pregnancy, but growing within you is another person, so the issue is not control of your own body, but that of your helpless little passenger.

"It's not convenient to have a baby right now." Ah, convenience; almost an American icon. Even parents who long for and plan their babies rarely find them convenient once they arrive. If my personal convenience were justification for murder under any other scenario, imagine the turnover in our courts!

"My birth control failed." Who said we have a right to behavior without consequences? If people aren't adult enough to accept that when they engage in certain behaviors, the natural result may occur in spite of their best preventative measures, they had best refrain until they

are grown-up enough to be responsible for that result a child.

"It would be unfair to the baby to bring it into (situation X)." Would it be fairer to the child to rip it to shreds, poison it with saline, or commit the ultimate in child abuse, a partial birth abortion? Would you, as an adult, care to be placed under similar lapses in logic and judgment?[11]

"I don't think I could go through with giving my baby up for adoption. "But, as in the scenario above, you could pay someone to brutally destroy a helpless, voiceless child, rather than give your baby a chance to live with a couple that has longed to have a baby. Yes, it is sad that you will not know who your child grows up to be, but you have this great comfort that you've given your baby the best gift: life.

"What about cases of rape/incest?" I was raped. Although the odds were against it, I became pregnant as a result. I was unmarried, just eighteen, and almost everyone I knew shook their heads and advised me to abort this child, and be done with it. I had no money, very little support, the rapist was from another race, and I lived in a very provincial, prejudiced area. It was most definitely not a convenient time in my life to have a baby. A lot of pressure was put on me by friends and family. They pointed out that I would never get to travel; work with art, theatre, or music; and that my life would be "ruined." I just cried, and said

"No, it won't be ruined, but it will be changed." I tried to think it out one thing at a time:

a. The rape was over, and nothing I could do now could make it not have happened.
b. The baby was a reality, and aborting him wouldn't somehow assuage me for reason #1.
c. The baby was innocent of any crime, his only offense – his existence! So executing a punishment – a cruel, capitol punishment at that – on an innocent child for the crime its father committed, seemed a rash miscarriage of justice.
d. Two wrongs don't make a right, and adding murder to a rape didn't seem like it was a wise trade either. A woman is likely to suffer far more from an abortion, than from rape, emotionally alone, not counting some of the horrific butchering of young women that goes on in "safe, legal, clinics."

"What about when the child, through prenatal testing, is determined to be less than "perfect," or has Down's or some other syndrome?" I have had three miscarriages, five children, and a few little experiences along the way. Long after Randy and I met, married, and had begun our family, I had some tests at the hospital that suggested trouble with our fifth child, Sara. The odds were very high that she would be a Down's baby. Well, we cried a little, then a feeling of awe began to envelope us: did God trust us so much that He felt confident giving us one of His special children,

who would need so much more? [The baby girl did not have Down's syndrome, after all, which also shows that doctors' fears are not always a good measuring rod for decisions.] You can have the perfect baby, take him or her to your wonderful home, and seven or eight years later, that child can fall out of a tree, or get hit by a car, and not be so perfect any more. Same thing for that handsome man of yours or your lovely wife; you can be thrown a curve - then what, people? Do you stick together, or fall apart?"

Randy and Donna continue to be thrown a curve to God's glory. Their lives are not easy, but they understand how precious life is and they are an encouragement to me.

Lastly, I think it is important to remember history. Growing up in Sweden we read extensively about Nazi Germany and the cruelties that were performed on the Jewish people in the concentration camps. Many pregnant women were used for research, their wombs ripped open; little babies were sometimes used for practicing target shooting among the German officers. Elderly people, people with deformities, the too young, the ugly, and the protesting, were dealt with swiftly in the crematories. Although this happened decades ago, it is repeating itself today in a more subtle way. The blood of the unborn cries even louder than history. Let us recognize that what is happening now is a repetition of World War II; the value of the weak is minimized, the methods of murder are cruel, and evil men (the executioners) go free, unpunished and even honored. The mother and the doctor (in many countries, the doctor in general practice also performs abortions), who were placed as the ultimate guardians for life, are the very ones making the decisions to terminate life. For the moment, God is forgotten. But He hears the cries. And as surely as He lives, that day will come!

CONTRACEPTIVES

> Do not deceive yourselves. If any one of you thinks he is wise by the standards of this age, he should become a 'fool' so that he may become wise. For the wisdom of this world is foolishness in God's sight.
> —1 Corinthians 3:18-19

Let's approach the core subject of this book. Compared to the rows of Christian books you could find on the subject of abortion, you might have to search hard for even one about contraceptives. They are out there, but have been limited to smaller publishing companies or home publishing (look through the reference index in the back of this book for more information). But like those authors, we will in the next pages try to speak plainly.

Because there is no support for limiting life in Scripture, the approval of contraceptives comes from reasoning. Most of the common arguments will be discussed in chapter six, *Common Sense*. Here we will deal chiefly with the underlying theory and motives for using them, as well as studying the modern methods of contraception.

What is Perfect Timing?

It is completely accepted, and seen as responsible, to nowadays plan when a baby should arrive. Actually, you will see parents become embarrassed if they find they are pregnant without planning it. "Ha ha, oops, mistake! Hi, baby!" So let us ask, what would be truly perfect timing, the man-made planning or the unhindered conception?

In the previous chapter we saw how God uses times and seasons to carry forth His purposes. Ecclesiastes 3:1 says it this way, *There is a time for everything, and a season for every activity under heaven...* We could read it in paraphrase, There is a right, a divinely appointed time for everything. And Solomon lists first that which is divinely appointed: the time for birth (Eccl. 3:2). It is very clearly seen in the birth of John the Baptist and the birth of Jesus who appeared in *the fullness of time* (Gal. 4:4). But even so, our lives were planned to enter time at a specific moment. God shows us very little in advance of when this perfect timing is, but we can make sure our children arrive on time by letting God dictate when conception happens. Divine timing is the first reason for not buying in to the popular spacing of children.

Secondly, God has a good reason for keeping some secrets of timing to Himself. He knows how easily we are tempted to find our security in plans and schedules and the knowing of when things will happen. Then our trust in God has no need to develop and we settle into a more comfortable predictability of life. It is easier to live with predictability than to trust God, with whom we wrestle with faith and doubt. When we do not trust that God does all things for a purpose, we fear the unknown. We desperately need to know and understand that God is in complete control, and that He will not somehow slip up in our lives. (It is somewhat comical that we trust Him so little, when we slip up all the time anyway! That should teach us that He can be trusted more than our own decisions.)

Having children transforms our lives completely! It changes everything; our work, our family, our time, our priorities. For those who want to control their lives, child spacing seems like pure wisdom and contraceptives seem the best invention in world history. But it leaves little room for a God who has a perfect time already in mind for conception but wants us to wait for the fulfillment without forewarning. Children will always be an obstacle to the five-year planner.

At the hard core junction of choice, I have no reasonable advice to give. The only thing I can say is throw out the plan, and keep your life open for God to work. Instead of a plan, He will give you a promise, and so grow your faith.

The book of Hebrews defines faith as *being sure of what we hope for and certain of what we do not see* (Heb. 11:1). Holding on to God's promises for us and stubbornly believing that they will be fulfilled will transform our very beings. Can I trust that all things will work for good in my life because I love God? Can I trust that I will lack nothing under His care, and that He will lead me right? Yes, I can (Romans 8:28, Psalm 23:1, 3). At some point we will stop worrying about the future. Instead, we will say, I don't know what the future holds, but I do know Who holds the future. Let the little children come.

THE MONTHLY NO

Drawing from God's Word that a child is a gift, I have been meditating on what that implies. I have already mentioned that God's gifts are unique and meant for our good. But what does it do to our relationship with the Lord when we deliberately refuse gifts He is trying to place in our hands? Let me illustrate with a story.

Here sits little Miss Mary, the five-year-old queen of her birthday party, in the midst of a delightful mountain of presents beside her. She is the envy of every eye in the room as she starts eyeing the pile for the present she will open first. She chooses the gift with the prettiest wrapping paper – silver stripes and stars. After opening the present, she looks at the gift with a little "Oh" and lays it to the side. Next, the biggest present of all is opened. "Oh, the doll stroller I wanted! Look, everybody! Thank you, Grandma!"

One of the children excitedly grabs their present. "Here, Mary, open this one! It's from me!"

Do You Dare Trust God for Your Family Size?

Mary takes a look at the wrapping and says in princess-like dignity, "No, thank you. It has green paper."

Mary's mother becomes embarrassed and quickly places the rejected gift in Mary's lap. "But you don't know what's inside, Mary."

"It's OK. I just don't want to open it."

"Remember somebody took a lot of time making this gift ready for you, sweetheart."

"Yeah. But I don't want it. I want to play with my doll stroller."

The girl with the rejected gift whispers, "My Mommy said you would really like it."

"I don't really want to open any more presents. I'm not interested in them."

Mary's mother is mortified at the behavior of her daughter, and the little girls surrounding her daughter try to deal with hurt feelings and stupefied wonder. How can she not want their gifts? She hasn't even looked! It was specially bought and wrapped for her! I will leave little Mary to finish her devastating party and then face her mother. We need to return to the world of adults with attitudes like little Mary's.

Children are gifts. God intended that particular baby to be given to that particular couple. Before the forceful attack on the value of human life, He found many couples who understood the greatness of what He was giving and they accepted the gifts gratefully and joyfully. It must be starting to wear on the heavenly Father to send good and perfect gifts just to find them returned unopened. Contraceptives became the Christian's acceptable way of declining divine gifts.

Many sincere and zealous Christians would probably like to argue with me, vouching for their sincere desire to please God in everything and that using contraceptives does not hinder their devotion. I do not doubt their sincerity, but I do say actions speak louder than words. What do you think? If you give a gift, is it not because you wanted to give someone something to show your love or appreciation? Is it not to give something that will benefit them or bless them? And your expectation is that the gift will be met with acceptance and joy. Let me propose that one of God's love languages is *giving*. He loves to give; He loves to surprise us with doing well for us, whether we deserve it or not; He loves to think out in detail how to give us extraordinary things. It should not surprise us to see Him pour out gifts on us, His bride, His beloved one!

It is very easy to please a natural giver. Simply accept the gift and he is satisfied. God is easy to please! With the accepting of the specific gift of conception, you have the privilege of carrying around in your body the obvious proclamation "Yes Lord" for nine months. Your one action of acceptance blesses the Giver for months! But, unfortunately, we also need to realize that contraceptives reject God's gifts every time they are used. Whether God intends to give you a baby or not, the contraceptive says for you, "No, thank you, God." I believe if we just had ears to hear, we would hear God say like Mary's mother, "But you don't even know what's in this gift." And He's got a point. We do not even know what we are rejecting! The Bible says it is something precious. Can you imagine the incredulous stares "Mac" would get if he rejected his $35,000 in prize money in *Who Wants to be a Millionaire* with a "No, thanks, I already have three grand in the bank?" Yet that is exactly what we do to God all the time!!

An abortion is a horrifying "No!" in the Creator's ears. But in His eyes contraceptives might be just as grave an offense for it is an ongoing act of slamming the door in the Giver's face. Every time a couple chooses to separate their lovemaking from producing fruit, it is a quiet and steady, "No, no, no, no, no..."

Some of you may want to come straight to the point and ask, "So, you're saying that to use contraceptives is a sin?" I will answer with another question: If God wants to create life in our family and we stop Him, are we working with Him, or are we resisting Him? It can be debated whether contraceptives are sinful or not, and it is not the object of this book to classify that. The real question in my mind is: Do we run the race to do God's *good, pleasing and perfect will* or are we half-hearted in our service? Do we love the Lord so much that we offer our bodies to serve Him (Rom. 12:1-2)? Carrying a baby is a very practical way for a woman to worship God and He is intensely pleased with it.

Motives

There are a multitude of different contraceptives and methods to choose from when a child is not desirable. Although some are more acceptable than others, we will go through the more common ones here. However, we do need to talk about the main issue of motive first.

The Lord loves children and we also need to learn to love them. Jesus said that He takes it personally; whoever receives a child for His sake can count it equal to receiving Himself (Matt. 18:5). That is no small promise! For a Christian, the question of *what* contraceptive to use is the wrong question. It shows a heart not in tune with the Lord's. The Lord's motive for creating marriage was so that He could receive godly offspring (Mal. 2:15). If we could talk to the Lord about contraceptives, we would likely find a blank stare or a pained look on His face and hear Him ask, "*Why* contraceptives?" The whole motive for contraception or abortion is to prevent Him from creating more life in our sphere of influence, and that is not His plan!

A common comfort for Christian couples who use contraceptives is that the Lord is Almighty and can overrule their actions. With the small chance of conception that is open with all medical contraceptives, they feel they have given the Lord a large enough window to overrule their actions, and a big enough wall to hinder nature from taking over. This was how my husband and I reasoned early in our marriage, although we still felt convicted of not leaving it entirely in His hands. As reality shows, most of the time the Lord chooses not to overrule. Why should He force His gifts on unwilling receivers? As in other areas of our walk with God, we choose how far we want to walk with Him.

METHODS

Let us now look at the different methods available and find out what they do. For the medical facts, I have briefly used Mary Pride's book *The Way Home* and refer you to that for further studies.[12]

Probably the most common contraceptive is the pill. Although there are many different kinds, some of them do act as abortifacient and not contraceptive. In the last few years Christian radio has made the Christian community aware of this. The pills do not only present a higher health risk for the woman using them, but they can also create birth defects in later wanted children.

The IUD's (Intra Uterine Device) also act as an abortifacient. There are some hair-raising testimonies from women who have been using these, in which they speak of how it caused great pain for them and, of course, for the few unwanted babies that survived.

The diaphragm and condom tend to make love-making more a farce than a romance. By trying to counteract what the sexual act is supposed to bring about (fruitfulness), they take away some of the joy and freedom of simply being together and unreservedly giving to each other. How much better to know that a baby will never be conceived without God's special purposes, and to have a blessed love life without sirens for caution going off every time!

Sterilizations[13] might be debated in the Christian circles, but they are very much present. Both for men (vasectomy) and women (tubal ligation) the sterilization is not at all risk free. For men, the sperm finds no way out of the body and must be tackled by the immune system. For women, there are great risks either of requiring a hysterectomy later on in life or contracting cervical cancer. I find it interesting that women may have wanted the sterilization in the first place to be able to get back in shape, only to find that the need for a hysterectomy later on spurred early menopause and aging. (My mother continued to look young through all her pregnancies, the last one in her mid-forties.)

For the Christian woman (or man), the greatest price with sterilization will not be the medical risks, however. It will be the realization that she has placed a curse of self-invoked barrenness on herself. Dee Smith shared in the magazine *HELP*:

> I underwent a tubal ligation in June, 1981. However, in June of 1984 the Lord began to deal with me. He showed me that what I did in essence was to have an abortion because I cut off the life which could have begun...As I shared with a friend (who also had a tubal ligation) what I knew, she seemed surprised and at the same

> time relieved to hear what was said. You see, the Lord had shown her the very same thing! Over the last few years, I have run into many other women who in trying to walk in a pleasing manner before God have also seen the same things in regard to sterilization. Most of these women have had other developments in their bodies which can be traced back to their tubal ligations. One major development is a sense of mourning and the lack of understanding as to why it's there. The mourning is for the babies who aren't in their lives...Read Deuteronomy 28 about the blessings and curses and you will see that barrenness is a curse–even a self-imposed barrenness...[14]

When the realization of being wrong hits, there is a remedy: reversals are available, but costly. But many couples consider it a small cost for a free conscience and for the chance to be blessed with a pregnancy again.

For many Christian couples, using a medical device to hinder pregnancy seems worse than more "natural" methods of stopping conception. Some women can feel when they are ovulating, or can calculate what time they are the most receptive, and the couple refrains from intercourse for a time. This can be excused with their common agreement to refrain, and that they are showing a godly self-restraint. But 1 Corinthians 7:5, talking about the marriage obligations, says,

> Do not deprive each other except by mutual consent and for a time, so that you may devote yourselves to prayer. Then come together again so that Satan will not tempt you because of your lack of self-control.

The only reason we are to refrain from the marriage bed is to devote time to prayer! Unless that is our motive, we have a clear command not to refrain. So, for the one method that should seem the most likely to have God's approval, He gives us a clear "No."

The second natural method is that of interrupted intercourse, where the man never lets the sperm enter the woman. The only specific Bible passage that speaks about this reads:

> Judah got a wife for Er, his firstborn, and her name was Tamar. But Er, Judah's firstborn, was wicked in the LORD's sight; so the LORD put him to death. Then Judah said to Onan, "Lie with your brother's wife and fulfill your duty to her as a brother-in-law to produce offspring for your brother." But Onan knew that the offspring would not be his; so whenever he lay with his brother's wife, he spilled his semen on the ground to keep from producing offspring for his brother. What he did was wicked in the LORD's sight; so He put him to death also.
> —Genesis 38:6-10

Onan had the specific task of producing offspring, but he was not willing and used the only contraceptive handy. That was reason enough for the Lord to kill him. With such an example of divine wrath, would we dare take the chance to call this an acceptable method? (You might say that Onan was explicitly disobedient, and it was for disobedience he was punished. Remember that we have not been freed from our charge to be fruitful either.)

So both methods that Christian couples might find more favorable or godly stand in complete contradiction to God's Word. For all previous generations that did not have medical devices, those were their options. Since God does not approve of them, I conclude He does not want married couples to find a way to stop fertility on their own.

Several mothers and authors who reject contraceptives still hold on to the natural contraceptive that God gave through nursing. I agree that the Lord made the woman's body wonderful in how it cycles through childbirth and the season of nursing. But, unfortunately, even nursing can be used as an excuse to prevent another pregnancy! The motive behind the action is still the same as for the woman who bluntly uses a medical contraceptive. If we are acting out of fear that nature will take over and pregnancy just happen, then we still have not learned how to trust the Lord. Why would we worry about nature when God is on our side? He is the Creator of nature and it can't do anything without Him! To some women God stakes out many months and even years after a baby's birth for no ovulation for His own reasons. It is His special design for her. For some, like me, the period has started right up after the normal blood flow following delivery and nursing does not keep us from receiving our next gift from the Lord. Others have to ask the Lord specifically for another baby before they can conceive. It is all individual and unique because God has different plans for each one of us. Freedom and peace come when we trust the Lord for His perfect timing. When it comes to baby-making, He cannot mess up, miss the right time, or give us too many by mistake. The God of the Bible is trustworthy, especially when it comes to creating human life, His own beloved image-bearers.

If I do, at times, lose focus on the Lord's glorious plans for me and my children, I joke about using the only contraceptive that is God-given *and* foolproof (and the only pro-life contraceptive there is): pregnancy! Did you ever think of that one? Once pregnant, I am covered from further pregnancy for the next nine months (and usually longer). It is impossible to get more pregnant than pregnant, so I relax and just enjoy the thought that it has happened, and I have allowed God to be in perfect control again. Any hidden anticipation (or worry) can be laid aside now that I know what's coming. I just pray for the new life and prepare to receive it. My heart has many months to ponder what little one God is so excited about creating in my womb. How blessed it is to have a new little *Yes, Lord!* on the way!

A Forgotten Tool of War

After looking at all the depressing ways we can avoid having children we can, with a sigh of relief, turn to a more refreshing subject: the free acceptance of them! When we stop fretting about the whole issue and turn it over to the Lord, we will find excitement and joy pouring forth from His Word in regards to the blessing of having children in the home. My favorite passage is Psalm 127 and the introduction of the full quiver. Here it is:

> Unless the LORD builds the house, its builders labor in vain. Unless the LORD watches over the city, the watchmen stand guard in vain. In vain you rise early and stay up late, toiling for food to eat - for He grants sleep to those He loves. Sons are a heritage from the LORD, children a reward from Him. Like arrows in the hands of a warrior are sons born in one's youth. Blessed is the man whose quiver is full of them. They will not be put to shame when they contend with their enemies in the gate.
> —Psalm 127

It really excites me to think about my children as arrows for my husband and me. You would think that if God wanted to make us strong warriors for Him, He would just add more spiritual muscles. Well, He will do that, but with His great vision for longevity (or shall we say eternity?), He more often chooses to give us children! Those sweet-looking little cherubs with fat cheeks and shiny eyes will some day, with the right training, send the whole enemy camp into confusion! (I can't get away from thinking about Jesus, the meek lamb of God, who turned into the mighty Lion of Judah and defeated Satan with one blow. Ha!)

There are many great things to look at in Psalm 127. Rick and Jan Hess gave us permission to share their discoveries from their book *A Full Quiver*:

> Now this matter of the "quiver." It originates from the Hebrew word pronounced ash-paw. For years I heard that the Hebrew quiver of Old Testament times held five or six arrows, and that satisfied me. It seemed to be an intelligent, if larger than average, limit. At least a lid was available for an otherwise nastily open-ended concept. Never mind that nowhere does God even *hint* at a limit of half a dozen.
>
> Well, several years ago, much to my astonishment, I heard an actual archeologist from the Middle East state matter-of-factly that the correct number of arrows was between twelve and fifteen!
>
> The reason pictures of ancient warriors etched in stone often showed five or six arrows per quiver was for the same reason that those warriors looked all alike. It takes far more time and dexterity to show lots of arrows in a tiny etched quiver than it does to sketch the idea of "many arrows" by just a few lines. You try etching fifty

warriors in stone sometime and see if you're not tempted to slim down the arrow quota!

A personal note here: I did not serve in the military and am, therefore, probably not a leading candidate for appointment to the Joint Chiefs of Staff. But even I have to admit that if I were a Jewish general in a heated battle with the Philistines, I would be much more confident if the members of my archery division each had a dozen arrows rather than just half or quarter that many.

To avoid any misunderstandings concerning the message of this book, realize that we are *not* stating that every couple must have twelve to fifteen children! Couples need only trust God to provide them with the perfect number of children for their situation. God can choose the ideal number for any couple. Let's just not base our thinking on a mythical six child maximum. The fact here is unarguable – a man with a full quiver, i.e., *the number he is supposed to have* is described by God as "blessed"![15]

Rick Boyer in his book, *Yes, They're All Ours,* also shares some thoughts worthy to be repeated:

> Scripture talks about several offensive weapons. There is the sword, for close combat. Then there is the spear, which can travel a certain distance or be used in close-up fighting as well. It's the arrow that has the longest range, along with a high degree of accuracy.

This is the thing that comes to my mind when I think of my children as arrows. I hold them in my hand for a while. I shelter them from the elements in my quiver; I make them myself and sharpen and straighten them. Then when the time comes to launch them they are prepared to strike targets that are far beyond my reach.

King David, mighty man of valor that he was, still had one target he wanted to strike before his life was over. His heart's desire was to build a temple for the Lord. But in Chronicles 17, God told David that that particular target was beyond his reach. The temple was built, but it was built by David's son, King Solomon after the death of David. David had not accomplished his goal in close combat but his arrow reached the target even when David was no longer on the scene.

I like the sound of that. In my life there are many things I would like to do for the Lord but which I will never accomplish. It's good to know that there are at least twelve children coming after me, all of whom I hope will be spiritually stronger than I ever was, are better educated and have more years left to serve God. Already my children can do important things that I can't do. I look forward to the future because I'm eager to see my arrows strike deep in the Lord's targets, accomplishing things for Him that are far beyond my reach.[16]

The Honored Man

What really encourages me with the thought of having and raising children is the hope and faith that they will be instruments in the Lord's hands, reaching farther than I ever could on my own. Like a seed buried in the ground, I sometimes feel forgotten or that my tasks are hindering me from doing great things for the Lord. But I know that as my little army of children grow to mature adulthood, they will show themselves to be the best investment I ever made! From enjoying the thought of a small family to accepting and allowing God to give more children, we stretch ourselves one step further. A desire is born to have a large family that we might excel in service for Him.

In 1 Chronicles we find that during the reign of King David, Asaph, Heman and Jeduthun with their families were set apart in the priestly service for prophecy. Heman had fourteen sons and three daughters and the sons seem to all have been serving the Lord prophetically. First Chronicles 25:5 states,

> All these were sons of Heman the king's seer. They were given him through the promises of God to exalt him [or exalt his horn, meaning increasing his power or influence].

God chose to give Heman this many children to honor him and make him mighty! Yet not everybody had large families. If you read 1 Chronicles 23:7-23, you will see that in the genealogies there is only one mention out of fifteen that had a great number of sons! Instead, we find many with one, two, three or four sons. God does not choose everybody to have big families. Having more than ten children was still the exception and a great honor from Him. But most families seemed to have more than two or three children.

Another passage that shows the glory of having a large family is Psalm 37.

> But the humble will inherit the land and will delight themselves in abundant prosperity.
> —Psalm 37:11

> I have been young and now I am old, yet I have not seen the righteous forsaken or his descendants begging bread. All day long he is gracious and lends, and his descendants are a blessing.
> —Psalm 37:25-26

For us who by faith have become Abraham's seed, we find that we and our children are part of fulfilling God's ultimate purposes for mankind:

> For I have chosen him [Abraham], in order that he may command his children and his household after him to keep the way of the Lord by doing righteousness and justice, in order that the Lord may bring upon Abraham what He has spoken to him.
> —Genesis 18:19

One of the reasons why we do not enjoy the thoughts of having a large family is because we do not understand the purposes God has in mind. There have been historical studies of the generations that have come from godly men and, not surprisingly, they show forth a wealth of blessed, productive men and women in high positions in society: lawyers, doctors, ministers, missionaries, government officials, and senators. Similar studies have been made for the posterity of wicked men and there was found a wealth of criminal activity, corruption, and untimely deaths. It will do us well to ponder this and ask God to release our children for His Kingdom work. God honors those who seek Him.

God's Gifts Can't Stop God's Plans!

A last little note before closing this chapter: I believe the Lord wants us to know that having children will never stop His plans for our lives. They require so much time, so much attention, so much training and disciplining, and so much love, that time for other activities and ministries must be limited while they are young. It does not mean that we are being hindered from service - we *are* in service continually. Nothing we do serves God better than investing in our families. But we will find our faithfulness in the task spill over into the lives of other people as we go along.

Know this: God's gifts cannot stop God's plans for your life, only your own plans can. The fear of being stuck with a bunch of children dissipates when we realize that it is the best and most meaningful thing we could ever set our hearts to do for God.

We also need to know this: training our children is more valuable in God's sight than to serve Him in any other office. This call goes out first of all to women, as men continue to serve in society to provide for their families and influence their surroundings (as we remember from the primary task principle). For us as women, while we have young children in our homes, it is good to know that caring for our children is far more important than serving in ministry duties as a pastor's wife or as a front-line missionary! For although the assembly line works quietly and without fanfare, little would be accomplished without it.

So I Can Serve the Lord Better

Enemy in sight!!!

Ready for battle!

Disarm him!

Secure the victory!

The weapons we fight with are not the weapons of the world. On the contrary, they have divine power to demolish strongholds. We demolish arguments and every pretension that sets itself up against the knowledge of God, and we take captive every thought to make it obedient to Christ.

—2 Corinthians 10:4-5

Confusion!

Raising children for God's glory is one of the best long-term investments we could ever make. It might even be the greatest one. Preachers encourage you to dream big for God; having children can be just that! By training them we extend our reach far into the future, where we personally can't go. By focusing our eyes not on what is directly at hand, but on God's purposes, we can deliberately plan to be a part of His work long after our strength fails.

I believe the Lord wants to move us into this vision so that we will be a people prepared for the future, with quivers full of strong arrows for the final battles ahead. At this point, it has not yet happened. The advocates for the small family still hold most of the votes. It holds Europe in such a grip that any family with more than three children is coldly stared down and given unkind comments. Although America with its voice for freedom has escaped some of the frozen attitudes of Europe, feminism has destroyed much of the old culture's heritage of love for children. Evidence of this is found in doctor's offices or in hospital delivery wards. Many hospitals have as part of their normal procedure, an after delivery talk to mothers about birth control! It is the perfect time to get the point across, "Congratulations! We share your joy - now stop it." And if we think these attitudes only permeate the secular West, we will have to think again.

The West was just a start; anti-life attitudes have marched around the globe and won votes. Hard though it might be to accept, many times it was the Christian laborers who brought the attitude with a westernized gospel. I discovered this personally while serving in a Muslim part of south Asia. The general Muslim population still believed in the blessing of having a large family, while the national Christians (who had been converted by foreign workers) had accepted the lie that having a small family was part of the Christian life, and they were proud of their enlightenment.

The Church's knowledge of God should have kept her out of trouble, but she has been deceived. You will find a great buzz of voices speaking up from within the church against abortion, and rightly so. But there is silence over the controversy of contraceptives, which continue to be widely used. Where are the voices of leaders who speak out God's desire to His people? What are the pastors, missionaries, leaders and ministers in the public light doing about this?

There are many exceptions, but a majority of Christian leaders have accepted this worldly norm, otherwise the objections would have raged! Having served within the mission ranks with team members from all over the world, I have been shocked by the lack of understanding shown both by leaders and team members concerning God's plan for the family. And who needs to understand this better than the one who desires to win people into God's *eternal* family?

The Lord gave missionaries (and, in fact, all believers) the task to present before an unbelieving world the true God, the Creator God, who created each person with love and for an eternal purpose; Jesus, the Lord of Life, who conquered sin and death; and the Holy Spirit, who indwells and gives life and light. It is all about life and what worth God puts on each of us! Why then do missionaries, of all people, go around the globe telling the Good News, while carrying in their bags contraceptives to prevent life from happening in their own families?[17] Somewhere along the way, the enemy came into God's field and scattered so much confusion about children that the truth was buried deep. This chapter deals with some of the major causes for confusion and I pray God will shed additional light.

WHAT DOES IT MEAN TO SERVE THE LORD?

Decide to serve the Lord today - become a missionary - go to the prayer meeting - sign up in the nursery! Utilize every second God gives you. For many, this is what it means to serve the Lord – to find good things to do. It is important to do good; we are called to it (Heb. 13:16). Yet if *doing* is emphasized, we easily forget that we are servants. A servant is hired to carry out his employer's plans and wishes, not to create his own agenda. A soldier serves his commander by following orders, and the commander counts on having the soldier's full attention at all times. Both the soldier and the servant think the same way, *What does my master want me to do? What has he already given me to be in charge of?* In the same way, I believe we can be a hindrance to God's plans by filling our schedules with "good works."

Jesus is our prime example. If doing good at all possible moments was the ultimate goal, the Lord's earthly life would have looked radically different. Do you realize He spent only three years in public ministry? How many times before that could He have had the opportunity to serve people's needs? Yet He waited patiently for His right time, faithfully working on menial tasks and serving as older brother in a large family. In Capernaum, He did not perform many miracles because of the people's lack of faith; He withheld His power. He did not call thousands to follow Him around in a personal school of missions; He chose just twelve. And think about the way He took time for weddings, food, and time alone with the Father. If He had chosen our age for his earthly life, He would have appeared to be a procrastinator! Yet He completely pleased the Father, and He finished His task on earth.

Busyness does not equal fruitfulness; it can actually hinder us from fruitfulness. It is very possible to do more for the kingdom of God in one hour of divine appointments, than in a full year of busy work. God's kingdom is heavenly. It is not bound by time, nor does it grow by human power, but is enabled by the Spirit. Satan tries to pressure Christians into busyness, while the Spirit gently draws them to the quiet place, where He infuses divine power. The one who learns to abide there does not hurry.

Do You Dare Trust God for Your Family Size?

Children take up a lot of time, and to serve them means to stoop to time-consuming, menial tasks. The idea has sprung up that children hinder serving the Lord. But apart from being part of service, they do not hinder anything that is significant in God's eyes, unless we decide to let a bad attitude rule the day. One missionary lady once asked a mother with little children: "Do you really think children are a better investment? You stay home all day, tending to runny noses and laundry, while I have a chance to share the gospel to several women every week." Both women served the Lord with all the understanding they had, and both will be rewarded in heaven. Yet knowing our God's rule over time, the first woman was mistaken. She equaled her time to fruitfulness. Just as easily, the Lord could send people straight to the other woman's door for ministry.

Another lady, a single woman on the foreign field, had worked hard for many years to see people won to the Lord, but with little results. The Lord prompted her to give Him her time. She decided to give Him every day until noon, and she spent that time with Him. She was scared at the thought of how much less she would be able to accomplish, but she stuck to her decision. Her co-workers went from shaking their heads to standing in amazement, as the Lord empowered her afternoons and let her see fruit from her labor.

I am not writing this as a call to stop working and just wait for God to take over. Jesus ministered to crowds when He was sad, exhausted, or hungry, without letting up until the task was done for the day. But the characteristic of Jesus' work was faithfulness, not hard work. And after the task was done He sent the crowd away and rested. That was faithfulness, too. There is a big difference between serving God in faithfulness and serving God with hard work. Here again, culture and human thoughts easily mislead us along the trail of trying to serve God in our own strength, and not by His Spirit (Zech. 4:6). Culture gives great respect to the hardworking person and we ourselves are prone to strive and push our way forward. But if we search our hearts, we will find that it is not for God's glory that we feel the urge to keep up the rat race. Our good motives for serving God get mixed with the hope of glory for ourselves, and we are driven forward by secret ambitions or fears. Our deceitful hearts betray us (Jer. 17:9).

Only Jesus had a pure motive and that was to please His Father by doing His will. Do you remember how Jesus called His burden light? A paraphrase of Matthew 11:28 could read, "Come here; you have wearied yourself out. My way of doing things is so simple that when you learn to walk in it, you will feel refreshed, light-hearted and at peace. Just come to Me and learn My way." If we seek only to do what God has given into our hands to do, the pressure of our own and others' anticipations will fall away. Then we can truly live faithful lives before the Father, and our service to Him will be a joy.

What Is True Sacrifice?

People who have a calling on their lives for full-time service often put this calling as the number one priority in their lives. And if full-time service in a certain field becomes the number one priority, having and raising children seems to interfere, rather than enhance God's work. In that view, limiting the family size seems the right thing to do. For some couples who fervently desire to be used by God in ministry, it can even take the shape of a great sacrifice, in which they give up having a normal family life for the sake of spreading the gospel. It is both great and heroic, surely something God must be pleased with. But consider the following:

> a. *There is no evidence in Scripture that we are supposed to choose our sacrifices before the Lord.* A sacrifice is the giving up of something we feel the Lord calls us to give up for His sake. Self-made sacrifices tend to be giving up something we do not really desire anyway in order to make us look great before men. The sacrifices God requires us to make are humbling and difficult. They go against personal desires, but extend hope for character refinement and eternal rewards. Human sacrifices tend to fit our abilities or circumstances while God's sacrifices often seem to make our situation worse and sometimes severely test our faith.

Entering missions as a teenager, I was contemplating making a vow to stay single for life. First of all, I had no great desire for marriage, and secondly I saw that my skills in language and culture adaptation could be of great benefit. The sacrifice was appealing to me. Later, when the Lord clearly pointed out that He intended for me to marry Jeff, I struggled for months. I couldn't see any glory for me in being a helper. I would much rather be on my own and do great things for the Lord! But at last my heart settled for obedience and trust, and I know now that *that* was a true sacrifice that pleased my Lord more than anything else I could have done. And the greater good that He promised me (Rom. 8:28) continues to unfold, my husband is my greatest catalyst for spiritual growth and clarity. And that is just the beginning of it! I am so grateful for the struggle, for now I know that I can trust God more than I can trust myself.

b. *To sacrifice having children is not to sacrifice ourselves, but someone else.* This is one strong reason not to believe that ministry is more important than having children. It is elevating our own service above the work of future generations. It is to forget that the same Creator who made us wonderful in all our skills will also make our children, and their children, and their children after them, wonderful and gifted. We would not be sacrificing just one child, but a whole lineage. Is such a view of our own importance godly, or prideful? And is the urgency of work worth such a great prize?

We need to go one step further. If by chance we still believe that to sacrifice children would be acceptable to the Lord, then we need to remember that He is Jehovah and He is the same today as when He revealed Himself to the Israelites. When He showed them the Promised Land, He warned them against the idolatry they would encounter. The worship of the gods Baal and Molech both involved child sacrifice and the Lord vehemently rejected this as evil and punishable by death (Lev. 20:1-5). In Jeremiah 19:5, God declares that child sacrifice is so remote from His mind and character that it shocks Him. We are not allowed to sacrifice anyone except ourselves, and we are urged to lay down our own lives for the sake of others –including our children.

Children should not be the sacrifice, but the Lord uses them to teach us much about true sacrifice because of their many needs! While we give them the chance to live and grow and become sons and daughters of God, He rewards us by teaching us to become less selfish and more serving. And that road will lead us in to His glory.

c. *True sacrifices have to be matched with God's Word and with obedience.* King Saul is a prime example of a man who decided to sacrifice to the Lord in a manner that suited him, rather than according to God's directions. The prophet Samuel had to rebuke him several times, and finally confronts him with the core issue of obedience:

Does the LORD delight in burnt offerings and sacrifices as much as in obeying the voice of the LORD? To obey is better than sacrifice, and to heed is better than the fat of rams.
—1 Samuel 15:22

To obey and trust the Lord can be difficult sacrifices at times. In most religions, great emphasis is put on asceticism and on sacrifice. But if we want to pour out more sacrifice to *our* God, let us consider the sacrifice of praise. Just to worship and adore Him and to draw near to Him is what He most desires (Ps. 50:14; 107:22). Think about this: do you believe God wants sacrifices, unless He has asked for them? (Ps. 40:6; 51:16)

I hope the above studies have been sufficient to convince you that having children is not to be cast aside as something insignificant. Having children is a sacrifice (and joy) the Lord most often provides to a couple. The one time it is a true sacrifice to not have children is when a couple is unable to conceive.

Do You Dare Trust God for Your Family Size?

Barrenness is very painful, and when the Lord does not lift it, He often has tasks for that couple that are of a special nature. What is surprising is that such couples often have a deep compassion for children and are more open to provide ministry to them, such as adoption, working with orphans, volunteering in the church nursery, or acting as foster parents or grandparents. It softens their hearts toward children, while voluntary barrenness hardens the heart.

Elisabeth Elliot writes in her leaflet, *Couples Who Choose Not to Have Children*:

> Number one, the first commandment given to Adam and Eve was to be fruitful and multiply. It's clear that marriage and fruit-bearing go together in God's mind. Number two, married couples within child-bearing age, of course, must hear God's call to parenthood. They may not opt out of this responsibility to Him, to family, to society, and to each other. Number three, to refuse to transmit life is to act against the nature of both man and woman as God designed it, and to ignore His plan.
>
> Christ never offered immunity; He asked for trust. Nothing in life calls for a deeper humility, a clearer recognition of our own inadequacies and helplessness, and a stronger faith than the gift of parenthood. It is calculated to put us on our faces in the dust. Shall we refuse the risk of this abandonment? Can we shut ourselves off from

the difficulties of motherhood and fatherhood and say no to sacrificial love?[18]

Who Is Important?

For by the grace given me I say to every one of you: Do not think of yourself more highly than you ought...
—Romans 12:3

Do nothing out of selfish ambition or vain conceit, but in humility consider others better than yourselves.
—Philippians 2:3

When the Lord shows us favor and hands us a great vision, it will be easy to think that our special service to God makes us more special than others. It is a basic human need to know our value, and I believe God has given us that need to help us find our home in Him. But the temptation is that we allow our ministry to dictate our worth and how much time and energy we can spend "on the side" helping others excel in theirs. This includes how much we believe we can invest in having and training our children. It becomes an evaluation in the dark, often short-sighted, as we calculate what is worth our time. "I am a gifted person; I know my ministry is important - am I supposed to sacrifice great chunks of it to help train my child?" Incorrectly, we tend to evaluate our ministry against the sacrifice of child rearing, rather than taking into account the future ministry and calling on the life of that child. But let us take a look at importance:

    a. *We all have an inherent value because God made us in His own image.* There is no difference between one human and another. We are all important. Yet the Bible also teaches that the nations that do not obey or acknowledge God are as nothing to Him; He has His heart set and places value on the people who trust in Him (Is. 40:17; 43:1, 4).

    b. *The one person is not important who does something important, but the one with whom God is pleased.* It works out that the one God is pleased with is the one He uses, and that person often becomes important in the public eye as well. But that is not always the case. Jesus told His disciples that if they sought to be important in His Kingdom, they needed to become servants (Mark 9:35). Servants do not work in the spotlight, but behind the scenes.

    c. *The righteous are importantly placed in history.* Once you begin to study and think about this, it will be hard to stop! To begin, Jesus came "in the fullness of time" (Gal. 4:4). Samson was foretold to become a man God would use, as was John the Baptist, Jeremiah, and others in the Bible. Almost as if in a divine chess game, God places His special ones strategically on the board to be ready for their time. Job was a masterpiece

He couldn't help but showcase; the obedient little girl Esther was fitted for her future as queen; the apostle, Paul, changed from a persecutor to an apostle, knew he had been made "a heavenly spectacle" (1 Cor. 4:9). But you can study any part of history after the time of the New Testament and find that God keeps playing His hand of people who change history for His glory. Now continue to study these important people; you will find that none of them sought that glory for themselves. They were honest, faithful and obedient to God. For many of them, their faithfulness was the very thing that led them into hardship and proved their worth.

We are placed strategically in history, too. We have an individual assignment from God to fulfill while on earth. But we will fulfill it by faithfulness, not by seeking out heroism for ourselves, nor hording time for ministry. If God wants to use us mightily, He will make it happen. If He desires for us to be His servants quietly, then that is how we will serve Him best. We will be important in His eyes either way.

d. *Children are historically important!* I hope you laugh at such an obvious truth! What would have happened to history if people in all other times could have hindered pregnancy like we can, and do, today? What would have happened if Leah decided she didn't want more than three sons? God would have had to find another ancestor for Jesus, who came from her fourth son Judah. And what if "high-risk" Rachel had decided to stop after getting her cherished Joseph? Benjamin would not have seen the light of day, and we would never have heard of Apostle Paul. What about King David? He was the eighth son.

I would give you a tour through history, to let you know how many significant people would be lost if their parents had counted it too great a cost to have more than three children, but a great compilation has already been made and can be found in Rick and Jan Hess' book, *A Full Quiver*, so I will not. All I will say is: "Praise God, George Washington and John Wesley, that your parents did not have such thoughts for themselves, either for leisure or grandeur, that they sacrificed you!"

e. *The unborn are important.* Past history, present time, or future history, they are all the same to the God who holds the time line. But to us, yesterday's men and women seem more solid, now that their deeds have been completed and recorded. But what about the future generations? Do we see them? Do we prepare for them? Do we love them, and do we allow them to come? If we are to esteem others as better than ourselves, does that not include our son or daughter or our grandchildren? Contraceptives have been accepted because they eliminate what we have not known; the child is as yet nameless and faceless. Because of selfish pride, we decide they are unimportant and not worthy to take into account. But he or she is the one that God is ready to spring into human existence. If the Holy Spirit stands ready to grant conception, we can be sure that the baby has already been planned since before the creation of the world and has an identity. About the fate of those souls who are denied entry into the womb, I do not dare to write, for it would be speculation. But I do know that to hinder a pregnancy is to hinder a person's entry into life, a very important person.

The Urgent Message

Another well-played card for confusion is the call for urgency. If you have been around many churches, mission agencies or revival meetings, you will have encountered it. *The harvest is ready and exceedingly great, the laborers are few, and the time is now! Throw aside all that hinders and join the gospel crusade!*

There is nothing wrong with this. Some people whom God is calling need that extra push and the invitation from the pulpit to take the challenge. For them, God's time has come. For others, it creates distress or guilt. They are also called to share the gospel, as are all believers, but their time is not yet ripe. They might be led to plunge into activity that has not sprung from faithfulness but from pressure.

In the same way, urgency creates exhaustion on the field. Reading too many biographies of heroes of the faith and forming a mental picture of what a hardworking missionary (or pastor) looks like can be disastrous. Instead of following the inner leading of the Holy Spirit, the worker tries his hardest to produce fruit through an intense schedule. In many instances, the lack of team members also creates an enormous surplus of work. It is so easy then for the worker to shoulder a burden God never intended for him to bear, and head towards burnout. The single most important skill that will keep a worker safe is discerning his personal calling and following it whole-heartedly, leaving all other things alone. Pressure and stress do not come from God, but from the enemy of our souls. Satan pressures us; the Spirit gently draws us.

The leaning toward contraceptives can be even stronger for the supported missionary than for those in the normal work world. The reason is that they are under such a commitment to work that they cannot handle the additional commitment to a growing family. The bitterest comment I have heard from an MK (missionary kid) is: "My Mom and Dad have time for everybody in the whole world, except for me." And why do the two seem so impossible to accomplish for them? Because it is more the rule than the exception that missionary wives are expected to fill some significant ministry role in addition to their husband's work, sometimes because of the work load, but many times to satisfy the sending/supporting group's requirements or wishes! The expectations are high for those who live on a support basis, and the pressure it creates can keep a missionary in the rat race and away from his true God-given tasks just as easily as if he had stayed home.

It takes great courage and wisdom to know how to walk faithfully to God's calling and to say no to other demands. It takes courage to trust God to care for you, your spouse, and your children. In short, it takes courage to be authentic.

Are Children Really in the Way?

My parents once heard an atheist declare that the meaning of life was to procreate the human race. When asked how many children he himself had, he confessed he had none. When it comes to acting on our words, the priority of the heart will reveal itself quickly. The man or woman who prioritizes work will feel hindered by all unwanted human contact. To them, it is a waste of time and an intrusion. Mary Pride writes in her book, *All The Way Home,*

> The same principles that have shackled Western missions have been carried over into the pastor's family, other church leader's families, and finally

all our families. They can be summarized like this:

a. God's work conflicts with family life.
b. God's work comes first.
c. Therefore, children are a burden that gets in the way of ministry.
d. So, children should be shuffled off to boarding school (if you are on the foreign field), or the nursery, baby sitters, or a program of their own (if you are at home) to get them out of your hair.

Let's not waste time deploring this. Let's state exactly why it is wrong, point by point:
1. God's work does not conflict with family life. Family life is where men are trained to be elders (1 Tim. 3:4, 5) and where wives are trained to be 'older women' of Titus 2:3 and 1 Timothy 5:10. The family is where new souls are brought into being and discipled in the most extensive way possible, while their disciplers learn by experience through this relatively easy job how to manage tougher disciples. Family life is God's work.
2. God's work of begetting and training children comes before institutionalized programs, nowhere found in the Bible, which take up the bulk of most churches' efforts.
3. Therefore, children are not a burden but the very soil in which church leadership grows. Not only do their parents gain

spiritual capital by taking this job seriously, but children brought up in such a household have a tremendous head start on converts from other backgrounds.
4. So if we really want our churches to grow, we should stop shuffling our children into corners and start helping parents to train their children in God's ways themselves.[19]

Children are not in the way. They require a lot of attention and a lot of care, and they seem to interrupt the most important moments with small requests and woes. But they do not hinder *God's work*. They help to remind us of what is truly important – to love – and so help us gain perspective on our other work. Children also remind us of our relationship with the heavenly Father. Almighty God is never too busy to listen to our smallest concerns and completely sympathize with us. He shows us that we are His priority.

What about the Lord Jesus? Did He let His work of preaching and healing disturb Him from taking time for children?

People were bringing little children to Jesus to have him touch them, but the disciples rebuked them. When Jesus saw this, he was indignant. He said to them, "Let the little children come to me, and do not hinder them, for the kingdom of God belongs to such as these. I tell you the truth; anyone who will not receive the kingdom of God like a little child will never enter it." And

he took the children in his arms, put his hands
on them and blessed them.
—Mark 10:13-16

Notice how the disciples found the appearance of children untimely as they were getting into great ministry opportunities at the Lord's side! The Lord was not disturbed at all by the children and their mothers, but obviously felt the need to correct the disciples' view on what was important to Him.

I see more and more that we are wrongly blaming children for being in the way of God's work, when it is actually we who are in the way. People are God's work. I'm reminded of the famous missionary remark, "I love serving God; I just can't stand people." In contrast Jesus said,

A new command I give you: Love one another. As I have loved you, so you must love one another. By this all men will know that you are my disciples, if you love one another.
—John 13:34-35

How much can we be used by God to minister His love if we are not willing to be inconvenienced for His sake? It is usually at the crossroads, the unexpected meetings or happenings, that God appoints us to minister. If we are not trained to respond with love and understanding, something else will spill out of us. Children will not hinder us from serving at those moments; in many ways they are the ones who will have trained us to face them. Only we ourselves can stop God's will from being done in our lives.

Whether in ministry or not, the basic task the Lord gives us after we get married is to care for and love our immediate family. There is no task in the Lord's kingdom that supersedes this while our sons and daughters are young. Tending to this basic task of life might actually be the very thing that will keep your family healthy and functioning for the long haul while you serve the Lord, keeping you from burning out or losing your vision.

A Question of Marriage

For all those whom the Lord calls into serious commitments in ministry, one of the questions they face and pray over is that of a life partner. The Lord intends some to stay single for life to serve specific purposes. For those intended for marriage, there is the need for a spouse who will serve the same life calling. Marriage is such a great part of life that God's servants need to be very certain of the Lord's direction in this area. Once the marriage vows have been completed, the Lord makes a couple as one in His sight. The priorities then turn to maintaining and developing this oneness and to producing fruit (having children).

From the time they enter marriage, the couple passes on the option of not having children, as far as the Lord would grant them. They have entered into a covenant with God to stay together to form a family, and God commands them to satisfy each other sexually (except for mutually agreed-on times of fasting and prayer). Rick and Jan Hess quote Liane Jablonski of Massachusetts, as she comments in *HELP* (issue number five):

> It is quite common for missionary couples to delay having children in order for them to concentrate on a specific situation that requires complete time involvement and/or to send the children they do have away to school for social and for work/time reasons as well. They often say that the only circumstance under which they would do this is for the Lord's work, which takes precedence over their own normal desires for family. It occurred to me that Paul addressed that subject, but his answer was not to not have children, but NOT TO BE MARRIED. In 1 Corinthians 7, Paul indicates that he believes being single is really the best way to concentrate on God's work, while allowing that being married is not wrong and is appropriate for some people. Since in the same chapter Paul definitely speaks against any length of celibacy within marriage (the only true reliable form of birth control!) maybe singleness should be (so to speak) the form that birth control should take for those who are truly in time-pressured situations, such as Bible translating/teaching for remote tribes when they are literally the only people (outside of the unsaved tribal people) who know the language and are Christians, and the guerrillas are moving in fast?[20]

Marriage is a package deal. It offers stability, marital fulfillment, and comradeship. It also requires faithfulness, responsibility, and willingness to be a parent. May every Christian man and woman be able to walk into this covenant with open eyes!

COMPETENT TO MINISTER

For the married man who desires to minister, there is a good reason why God wants him to have children; it is part of the process God uses to mature him and make him an effective and faithful follower and leader. First Timothy chapter 3 gives instructions on what kind of men should be established as overseers and deacons. They were chosen upon observation of their family life and reputation, not because of their gifting and skills.

> Here is a trustworthy saying: If anyone sets his heart on being an overseer, he desires a noble task. Now the overseer must be above reproach, the husband of but one wife, temperate, self-controlled, respectable, hospitable, able to teach, not given to drunkenness, not violent but gentle, not quarrelsome, not a lover of money. He must manage his own family well and see that his children obey him with proper respect. (If anyone does not know how to manage his own family, how can he take care of God's church?) He must not be a recent convert, or he may become conceited and fall under the same judgment as the devil. He must also have a good reputation with outsiders,

> so that he will not fall into disgrace and into the devil's trap.
> —1 Timothy 3:1-7

The man described is not young and inexperienced. He has had years of maturing a good, solid character and has earned a good reputation by continual faithfulness in training his children and avoiding excessive habits.

When I was growing up, I thought my Dad was a model of patience. I am realizing now that he learned how to be faithful because, otherwise, he would have been constantly frustrated! He answered a thousand questions a day, sorted out hundreds of squabbles between siblings, and was the constant judge in all minor and major conflicts. Almost every waking hour he spent at home he was teaching, training, admonishing, comforting, explaining, rebuking and commanding his growing army of kids. He was my example of Jesus through my teenage years with his gentleness and patience.

There are few things in life that drive us to the Lord like felt needs. I have not felt a greater need for character refinement than after I became a wife and mother. The training in patience, unselfishness, gentleness and self-control is intense! But without my husband and my children, I would not have grown fully in these areas.

Without the intensive training that family provides for the man or woman of God, there is a good chance that some character growth has not had a chance to happen. Even if the maturity is there, family life is supposed to be an indicator for measuring one's faithfulness in God-given tasks. If a couple has cut short the intended number of offspring for the sake of service, part of the test for being established as a leader has not been completed. Should we promote to professor he who on purpose has been foregoing part of his exams?

DREAMS, SKILLS, AND DESIRES

I want to address wives of ministers as well as Christian women in general. We live in a time and age where many of us are able to obtain an excellent education and have promising career opportunities available to us. If we are talented in a certain area, we are often encouraged by those around us to pursue the stars. The Lord Himself has put into our very souls the desires and dreams that are just waiting to be unlocked and fulfilled. At some point in life, we begin to put all these things together to form an understanding of what God has planned for our lives. Our hearts want to settle into a life work, which fits us perfectly and brings out our passion.

Many of us find that, when we are married, our life pursuits conflict with our new mandate to care for the needs of a husband and children. We realize that God's order is in opposition to what we have learned from living in the midst of our modern culture. Culture tells us, "You can have it all," but that focus is on fulfilling our dreams. God, on the other hand, places us as a helper to another person, and our primary role is to serve. It should not come as a surprise when young wives and mothers struggle with their new roles in the home. Many times their hobbies and interests are laid aside to care for their families, while the dreams they thought were from God now seem unattainable. Those with the gift of evangelism are ashamed they are not out winning souls, those with compassion for others feel guilty that they are not caring for people in the community and those with the gift for teaching are upset that their skills and minds are being dulled by chores. Until they come to peace with what God is doing with them, they will find themselves at the crossroads of many difficult questions and decisions.

What is God's will? What is my part to choose? Has not He who created me also given me a great mind and made me able to succeed in a vocation? What about my dreams of being able to serve my community? When other people acknowledge my abilities and know I can go far in my field, would God give me this much and then just desire that I be a housewife and numb my mind with the daily chores of life? It doesn't make sense.

Fears are hiding underneath those questions fears that we will not be fully used for good purposes, that we are too insignificant for God to care if we are unfulfilled or left out, that we will not have a full chance to grow and bloom. But those fears can be dispelled if we come to know God's promises and realize that we can trust Him completely for our future. We carry in our very core the desires that God planted in us even before we were aware of them. He planted them there so that we would be moved to act according to His good will. Not all desires and dreams come from Him, but we can discern which ones are from Him by their persistence and by their goal of manifesting God's glory. He does not ask us to give up those dreams, but to nurture them. For instance, if we dearly desire to help needy people, we can be sure it is a God-given desire as it is the Holy Spirit wanting to manifest the character and compassion of God through us. Without the nudging of the Holy Spirit, we would never care for others that way because the sinful nature is too occupied with a focus on ourselves (selfishness). Such desires and dreams are good, but just like seed, they will not be ready to be revealed until God's purposed time comes. We are set to watch over the seeds, but the main thing we do is wait.

> Trust in the LORD and do good, dwell in the land and enjoy safe pasture. Delight yourself in the LORD and he will give you the desires of your heart. Commit your way to the LORD; trust in him and he will do this: he will make your righteousness shine like the dawn, the justice of your cause like the noonday sun. Be still before the LORD and wait patiently for him.
> —Psalm 37:3-7

> But seek ye first his kingdom and his righteousness, and all these things will be given to you as well.
> —Matthew 6:33

> Who then is the faithful and wise servant, whom the master has put in charge of the servants in his household to give them their food at the proper time? It will be good for that servant whose master finds him doing so when he returns. I tell you the truth; he will put him in charge of all his possessions.
> —Matthew 24:45-47

There are two ways of going about the Lord's business. One is trying to take charge of what the Lord has promised us and to do it without waiting for His timing and direction. The other is to wait while holding on to the promise God has given us.

The task of caring for our children is long and sometimes exhausting, but the wait provides a time when we can prove ourselves faithful in what the Lord has already given us. As we take up that challenge and see the Lord provide us with grace and strength at home for all the daily tasks, we can grow in confidence that He will provide for us and equip us for any task ahead. I believe the time of waiting is what makes us ready for the desire of our hearts to be fulfilled. It is not something we can skip over to get to the more exciting parts of life faster. The Lord may allow us to wait a long time for His promises to be fulfilled, but they will be (Heb. 10:23). While we wait, He will use our faithfulness and make us useful right where we are—in the midst of our training. Finally we will see our desires take shape and bloom, but it may be in a different way than we anticipated. Such a ministry that has been sown by tears, years, and persistence will grow strong and bear fruit.

If we decide to stay home with our children and trust the Lord with our dreams, we may or may not be involved in the professional world—the Lord alone knows whether that is part of His plan or just a projected idea that stems from our desires. One thing is sure—in His good time we will flourish in our skills and be fulfilled in our desires, if we will wait for Him and closely follow His direction.

A Family Ministry

We have studied both the husband's and the wife's roles in ministry and in marriage. We have personally received a calling and a disposition from the Lord to perform the work He has planned for us. The picture would not be complete unless we also mentioned the family vision that God wants to infuse in us.

In God's kingdom everyone works together: the Father, Son and Spirit; the Head and the body of Christ; the husband and the wife; the servant and the Master. While the home is full of children, they are part of the vision carried by the parents. The missionary may find that his young son has greater freedom to witness than he has; a musician finds that her daughter strengthens her impact by her singing; an intercessor discovers allies in his children. The Lord continues to give spiritual gifts and skills to children that enhance the gifts of the parents. The children are also naturally trained in the qualities the parents exhibit as they observe and take to heart what their parents value and emphasize. Thus, the strength of the parents becomes even greater with the addition of the children and their gifts. The evangelist who loves talking to people on the streets about Jesus may wake up with amazement fifteen years later and see that several of his children have become skilled evangelists and are eager to accompany him! Children who respect and love their parents cannot help themselves; they just love what their parents love. And even if a child would seem as different as could be from his parents, he will bring new things into the family storehouse. The study of the natural family – the family grown without the interruptions of contraceptives or selfish pursuits – is fascinating and inspires awe. I pray God will continue to reveal His glorious plans, so that we will be moved to become His willing people.

Chapter Five

Common Sense

The wisdom of this world is foolishness in God's sight.

—1 Corinthians. 3:19

Overcoming Reasoning

There are many reasons why people decide to postpone childbearing. Medical problems, financial security, finishing education, and family expectations come back over and over in casual conversations between friends. These reasons usually win full approval and continue to establish what culture labels as responsible planning.

We are all humans. Reasoning makes sense to us. It is not until God illuminates our hearts with divine truth that we come to realize that reasoning often leads us astray. Why is that? To *reason* means to try to make sense of something, to find an answer, or to find our way. Usually our minds reason when we have not taken God into account. If we do not take God into account, the one who has made everything for His own purposes, we end up with faulty answers.

In this chapter, we will look at common reasons why Christians choose to use contraceptives. Although many of them can be answered by revealing information that ought to be common, it is the heart attitude behind these decisions that needs to be addressed. For many couples, their lack of interest in children is simply a product of their lack of understanding of God's involvement in their lives and His main purposes. We need to return again and again to the main question: can we trust God completely? Can we trust Him for our bodies, for our health, for our family size, and for our daily needs?

Once we find an answer to that question, there will be no more need to reason. Faith is enough, as stated in the following Scriptures:

> This is the victory that has overcome the world, even our faith
> —1 John 5:4

> ...the one who trusts in Him will never be put to shame.
> —Romans 9:33

HOW MUCH CAN WE AFFORD?

"The government recently calculated the cost of raising a child from birth to eighteen and came up with $160,140.00 for a middle income family. Talk about sticker shock. That doesn't even touch college tuition."[21] (And after hearing that, you look around and are surprised to see that there are still children around!) Mary Pride writes, "We are the richest people in history, yet the most fearful about the costs of child-rearing. Perhaps it's because we don't realize how super-fatted our lifestyles are, and how little our children really need in order to grow up happy, healthy, and godly."[22]

When the heart is set to the task, there are a million ways to reduce costs. Money, to some degree, is but a reflection of the steward/spender. What the believer discovers to his joy is that God claims ownership over his life, with all its responsibilities. He is not dependent on our finances! It might be

Do You Dare Trust God for Your Family Size?

good to remind ourselves that the money systems were not set up by God, but by man. They helped people establish a price tag on their possessions or their work, and served to help people amass or identify their material wealth and position. But as children of God, we are set above this human system as we lean on the provisions that the Lord sends – He determines whether it comes through steady paychecks or through other means. True value comes from God. He is Jehovah Jireh, the ultimate Provider. God's children often have their needs met in unexpected ways, not the least through the hands of other believers. The giving of tithes is a great example of how God's blessing is the thing that secures our provisions.

> It is the blessing of the Lord that makes rich, and He adds no sorrow to it.
> —Proverbs 10:22, NASB

My parents experienced this in many ways. They raised sixteen children on my father's salary as a teacher and on the Swedish national child support (given to all families in the country, as a monthly tax return). Whether little or much came in, at the end of the month the money was always gone. When they learned the secret of giving money to the Lord's storehouse (tithing) the Lord put His blessing on their material goods. The washer, dryer, dishwasher and family vehicle did not break down, everyone stayed healthy, and food was plentiful. When Sweden removed some of their support to large families, my parents lost a substantial part of their yearly income. But strangely enough, I could not detect any lack or difference on our table. There was still plenty. When finances became tight, my parents sometimes decided to stop tithing. Then things started going wrong; a machine would break down, important keys were lost, the van needed repairs. In no way was God acting capricious, but He was serious when He stated, *Test me in this. When you give Me what is Mine, I will bless you* (Mal. 3:8-12). So as I grew up, I had a first-hand lesson in trusting God above money.

Think about it. *It is the blessing of the Lord that makes rich, and He adds no sorrow to it.* If it is God's blessing that makes us rich, and children are a blessing from Him, I do not see that we have any reason for worrying about the cost of having them. Instead, we might wonder if we can afford not having them!

In Matthew 6:25 Jesus states this:

> Therefore I tell you, do not worry about your life, what you will eat or drink; or about your body, what you will wear. Is not life more important than food, and the body more important than clothes?

Then He goes on to promise us that all earthly needs will be met as we look to the Father. In Psalm 127:2-3 we find that children are not meant to be a financial burden on the family father:

> In vain you rise early and stay up late, toiling for food to eat - for He grants sleep to those he loves. Sons are a heritage from the LORD, children a reward from Him.

When we commit to having and raising children for God, we ultimately place the responsibility for their welfare in His hands. Although we are stewards doing all in our power to care for them, at the end of the day God is the only one who can completely sustain them and provide for all their needs. And that is exactly the point to which God wants to bring us - completely allowing Him to be in control of us and of our children. We allow Him to do His work His way.

What is Responsible?

It is ironic to me that culture often labels parents of many children as being irresponsible. A society without God as the foundation sets up its foundation on uniformity, predictability, and careful planning. Life without God means someone needs to be in control. It has been encouraged for almost a century that families need to become smaller and their living standards higher. Couples who follow that pattern will be viewed as being responsible in society. Those who do not conform will be considered irresponsible and experience pressure.

As God's children, we have been set apart to serve another kingdom, with a completely different set of basic rules. We are not meant to live up to both standards. Jesus reminded His disciples of this before facing the cross:

> If the world hates you, keep in mind that it has hated Me first. If you belonged to the world, it would love you as its own. As it is, you do not belong to the world, but I have chosen you out of the world...If they persecuted Me, they will persecute you also.
> —John 15:18-20

To be in conflict with a godless but accepted norm is not bad; it reveals that God is helping us overcome the world system and its hold on our thinking.

What matters for us as believers is what our heavenly Father thinks of us. Are we responsible in His eyes? It is enough to glance back at the basic command to realize that God would never call us irresponsible for having children, however many. He is sending them to us that we might care for them. And if we do accept the charge and care for them, we will be called *faithful*. And who does not want to be described that way when the Lord embraces us on that wonderful, coming day? *Well done, good and faithful servant!* (Matt. 25:21)

Sometimes I remember how the world labels me as a stay-at-home mother of many: crazy, sex maniac, baby drooler, enslaved, sentimental, out-of-control. "A baby a year! You've got your hands full!"

But I don't dwell on that too long. Instead, I remember what my own father once said to me with love and admiration, "God really trusts Jeff and you with a lot of responsibility." And my Dad is but the echo of the voice of my heavenly Father. God trusts us! He trusts us to be faithful to fulfill His plan and that is exactly what we desire.

Having children is a high-level responsibility from the Lord. He entrusts us with a small person's physical, emotional, mental, and most of all, spiritual well-being. Just as a missionary is sent out with a call to bring lost souls home, so the parent is called to train the child to embrace the love and plan of God. The Lord has given parents a great deal of power to build or destroy their children while they are young. When we see and hear about all the abuse that occurs, we might wonder *why* He entrusted it. But for the loving parent who walks with God, he or she is the best representation for the child to know what He is like. However much we may try to avoid it, we cannot; we are His image-bearers, and we reflect Him. When we do not reflect Him well, we distort our children's view of Him. The responsibility is therefore to daily reflect Him and pave the way for our young ones to come to know and love Him. It's such a great task - and such a great privilege!

When it comes to the question of responsibility, let's check out who is talking. Often the ones with the most advice are those who have not understood that God prioritizes children way above most other works. We gently, but firmly, must stand against this misconception so that the Lord may have His way in His people.

"I Need to Care for My Body and My Health."

You might have heard that a woman's body needs about two years to be fully prepared for another pregnancy. I am sure there is some soundness in this statement, for often this is what the Lord grants a woman after childbirth. But as with everything else in the realm of walking with Almighty God, a man-made statement should not be allowed to frighten women from having children. We can completely trust God with our bodies and with our health. He knows us completely. If the truth is confirmed in our minds that children cannot arrive unless He is directly involved, we also know that He sees us fit to handle the task. I have had one child every year since Jeff and I were married in 1997. This is uncommonly close in most families, but the Lord has granted it to us. The amazing thing that I have experienced is that about two months after delivery the emotional veil of pregnancy, delivery, and nursing usually lifts, and my body feels restored again. The thought of another pregnancy becomes exciting and not exhausting. The more I embrace the Creator's plan for the continuing of the godly seed (not meaning Christ, but Christ's little ones), the easier it is to accept the sacrifice of my body to the Lord. I also gratefully acknowledge that He gave me the desire to have children after I surrendered my will to His plan. I believe He will do the same for anyone who asks Him.

Some speak confidently of the detriments to a woman's body that comes with pregnancy, but they forego the greater harm that comes through the use of contraceptives. Although pregnancy takes a toll, this is something the Lord programmed a woman's body to handle with His help (Gen. 4:1). Mary Pride points out in her book *The Way Home,* that medically it does a woman good to have children and hindering pregnancy takes a greater toll in the long run than a pregnancy does!

I do not deny that there is a cost in childbearing; however, there is a divine reason for this. It helps us to focus on Him and not on ourselves.

> Therefore, since Christ suffered in His body, arm yourselves also with the same attitude, because he who has suffered in his body is done with sin. As a result, he does not live the rest of his earthly life for evil human desires, but rather for the will of God.
> —1 Peter 4:1-2

The Lord does not promise us ease. But for every time He commissions us and we accept it, He protects us with a whole arsenal of divine promises! For the man and woman who walk in faith there is no need to fear sickness, too heavy a burden or detriment. Instead of trusting in a life insurance plan, we can lean on the Life-Planner's assurance: *No harm will come to you that I do not ultimately turn for your good* (Rom. 8:28).

The Western culture has forgotten God as Jehovah-Rapha, the Lord our Healer. Although medical care is good and needed, we have access to the great Physician Himself and we can trust Him more than a doctor's touch or a prescription. We are also comforted by remembering that He is the God of miracles, and that He is the same as He was when He parted the Red Sea, raised the widow's son from the dead, and conquered sin and hell (Heb. 13:8). We are on the winning team!

There will be many women who have been given advice for health reasons not to have any (or any more) children. A man and wife will prayerfully consider what the Lord is saying in that situation. It is not an easy decision and this book is not meant to deal out advice from a comfortable corner. God alone knows the situation. But we know this; he who trusts the Lord through greater trials also receives a greater reward. Job said in his misery,

> But He knows the way that I take; when He has tested me, I will come forth as gold.
> —Job 23:10

When you look to Him, when you hold on to faith, what do you believe you should do? Follow that path.

Quality Time

Some people say they can not have more than one or two children because they feel they could not take care of them properly or spend enough time with them as individuals. The problem is usually not the children, but the fact that the mother is working outside of the home. Many times couples choose to have only one child because the mother wants to pursue a career, and that in turn leads to her dilemma of not spending enough time with that child. A mother who is home all day can take care of ten children and still spend time with each of them for she is stationed, and they know where to find her. However special it is with quality time, their need is for the whole day, and for all seasons, not just for good times together.

There is not enough time for a woman to go to work from nine to five while her children are small. Children grow too fast. That job outside the home can never match the influence a mother has on her children. She is the one who can impact them and purposefully raise them with God's plans in mind. The financial gain cannot compare with such a task.

"We Need Two Incomes to Make It"

I hear this often from women who work outside the home. I do not believe this is a valid argument for a woman who has entrusted herself to the Savior. God has repeatedly said in His Word that He will provide for those who belong to Him and trust in Him. Jesus told us to seek God's kingdom and His righteousness first, and that all our needs would be met (Matt. 6:33). He has said that He grants sleep to those He loves, and that it is in vain that we labor hard for income (Ps. 127:1-2). It is impossible for a trusting child of God to starve.

One thing I noticed when I began my higher studies in Sweden, was that Satan was using the school system to try to keep me away from God and from meditating on the things of God. School began early in the morning and continued until late in the afternoon. Afterwards, there was so much schoolwork to do and so many tests to study for, that I went to bed late at night. The next morning I would be so tired that any time of prayer turned into a time of dozing. The USA is no different. Satan is playing this card frequently in all of our lives. Husbands have to spend more and more time at work, children spend longer and longer hours in school or daycare (away from their parents, to whom God gave the command to train them), and women are enticed into the work place. It might seem like you need the extra income, but it is a smoke screen. You need God to give you the miracle of divine provision, and it will only come as you stay on your post and keep trusting Him for it.

What do people mean when they say *make it*? Usually it does not mean basic needs. When Jesus preached the Sermon on the Mount (Matt. 5-7), He identified our three basic material needs: food, clothing, and shelter. We could say our basic needs are met when we are at a level where we can function well as human beings. Well, the real level is far below what even poorer families live with in

Do You Dare Trust God for Your Family Size?

the States. The problem is usually not the lack of funds. The problem is discontentment. We live on a super-fatted lifestyle, demanding to have every little desire (boosted by constant advertisement) fulfilled in an instant. Just because we are used to certain luxuries does not mean we really need them. This was vividly illustrated to me while living in Kabul, Afghanistan, during the last year of the Taliban regime. We often found starving people begging at our door. Ignorantly, I imagined us giving out beautiful care-packages with nice food items they could not afford themselves. Our doorkeeper shook his head disapprovingly at my idea and said: "No! Give flour, cooking oil, rice and tea." Those were the only things they counted as essentials. In the wintertime many families needed blankets and winter clothing. Some desperate families needed help paying their rent. Food, clothing, and shelter; they seldom asked for more. And there we were, from a wealthy nation, feeling almost starved from the lack of normal American luxuries, while the Afghan people believed we lived like royalty. Talk about culture shock!

Though it would be nice to write that God has promised us at least an average American income, it would not be true. He promises to provide for our needs, and to bless us. And for many of us, He tests our trust through finances.

I grumbled a lot when my husband went through Bible school. At the time, we had two small children and I stayed home with them. My husband went to school in the morning and to work in the afternoon.

The partial income with the large school bills left little money for food. We found a food store with affordable prices, but I was angry and bitter as I slimmed my weekly grocery list down to the essentials and went shopping with my ten dollars. It proved to be enough! As I drove home, I was so ashamed of my attitude and lack of trust, yet at the same time, was so full of gratitude to a God who cared so personally for us. We never starved and most of the time our cupboards were quite full. God tested us, but He also blessed us.

All the bills, debts and desires that accumulate will try to force a mother to work. God does not. With wise handling of one income the family can go a long way. Money is not the true source of income. God is.

Rabbit Tales

Although I touched on this before, this is a rabbit trail I want to follow up on. Charles Darwin managed to confuse the world with his book *The Origin of Species*. Instead of accepting that there is a Creator behind our structured universe, he allowed for chance to become god instead. He stipulated that the earth was formed by accident, all living things stem from one giant coincidence, and that humans are, as all other beings, just part of the food chain. In other words, we are nothing special. We simply exist and reproduce; we raise our children, they exist and reproduce, and the cycle continues. That's it, folks.

In a nation where God is acknowledged, that falsehood still crept in. People are like rabbits; if you leave a couple without proper protection, they will reproduce. God was the Creator, and He put the reproduction machine in motion. Now it seems His role is just watching it go. People are afraid to let go of the control, because they do not see that God is in direct control over their fertility, and without contraceptives, they would all too quickly multiply!

As we saw in chapter two, this is a very faulty view. God has not set up the universe and all natural laws to run without Him; instead, it says that He is *sustaining all things by His powerful word* (Heb. 1:3). If He let go, all would fall apart! And likewise, there would be no conception unless God's Spirit was there to grant it. Because His Word says that He planned our lives before the beginning of the world, there is no room to think that He is a passive bystander when a child is born. A gift comes from a giver.

So, no more rabbit tales. Even the poor rabbit would not be able to have bunnies if the Creator did not grant them. It just so happens, that God loves bunnies, and children too. He intends for them to be born and to live.

"I Would be Bored at Home"

For a working woman, the thought of becoming just a homemaker is sometimes equated with boredom. Even if her job is nothing more than a routine office job from nine to five, this has been viewed as superseding staying at home with one's own children. The feministic movement believes so strongly in its cause, that any employment position, even the worst, is better than staying at home. They have forgotten that woman was the one who first defined home for what it is supposed to be. True, sometimes being at home can be boring, but it is a statement that is self-fulfilling. With a new outlook on what children mean to God, the value He places on motherhood and faithfulness, and how in everything He promises all will work out for good, being at home can become the most fulfilling place for a woman. Allow me to explain why.

If you are a housewife, or considering it, let me suggest that boredom comes from not being in a place of fruitfulness. Taking that one step further, the only place of lasting fruitfulness is in the place God especially designed for you. I believe as strongly as those who proclaim that women should be able to take any position, that God gave you unique gifts and intends to use them for His special purposes. But it has to be within His boundaries! God does not overstep His own plan just because our culture changed, and now it's acceptable for women to work outside the home. He has designed you to work *from* your home.

One time I did something that transformed my life. I made a list of what God had entrusted to me; responsibilities on assignment from Him. The idea came from reading the book, *A Woman after God's*

Do You Dare Trust God for Your Family Size?

own Heart by Elizabeth George. I wrote down on a paper seven areas of my life where I needed to learn to be faithful and consistent in well-doing; God, Jeff (my husband), my children, myself, home, friends, and ministry. I sorted them in the order of priority. Then I wrote under each area what specific things I needed to be faithful in. For example, under *God* I wrote: Daily time with Him, obedience, practice His presence, prayer, thorough Bible reading, and studies. Under My Children I wrote: Prayer, train in godliness, healthy and happy, love and discipline, taking time for them, care for needs. And so on with the rest. These were all practical things I could do. I went back frequently, noted what areas I did not do well in and prayed for the Lord to change me. As the days went by and I worked only within these seven responsibilities God had given me, I saw that I had time for nothing else. There was no time to sit and watch TV, read novels, or talk on the phone for very long. And there was no time to be bored! Instead, as I worked and I began to notice how God was changing my attitude and gave me a heart to do what He wanted me to do, I began to rejoice! It became a joy to start the day. Instead of anger or frustration at being stuck at home, and figuring God can't use me for anything better, I saw how I was fulfilling His plan for me and for my family. I was learning faithfulness, love, and service, in a place of grace and acceptance. No one criticized my mistakes. I was growing in the Lord, and I felt my spirit *soar like an eagle*—so free, so released. But it didn't stop there! Once I noticed that my responsibilities were being fulfilled faithfully, my heart began to ask for more. I asked the Lord to increase my boundaries according to His Word, *He who is faithful in little, more will be given.* So He gave me more opportunities that I could grow in and serve Him with. I was freed up to serve because I had learned what my priorities were.

There is no boredom when we are about God's business. There is fulfillment, and enough exciting work to satisfy any workaholic or encourage any lazy mind, yet a wonderful rest that comes from a peaceful heart. For me, the best thing is to be able to rest in the knowledge of doing exactly what God has called me to do, without any shame, and with no big missed opportunities.

> Who then is the faithful and wise servant, whom the master has put in charge of the servants in his household to give them their food at the proper time? It will be good for that servant whose master finds him doing so when he returns. I tell you the truth; he will put him in charge of all his possessions.
> —Matthew 24:45-47

Watch out world! For to a faithful servant He entrusts all He owns!

"But What About My Life?"

It is true that people find fulfillment when operating in their gifts and skills. God designed us to experience a special sense of pleasure when we shine in our tasks. There is truth in what culture says, *Listen to your heart. Do what you like to do. Do what you are good at.* But it is just a half-truth. Who has not experienced the immense pleasure and intoxication from working on a special project, only to form a depressing evaluation later, "What is it all for? Why have I spent so much time and effort on this?" The answer is simple. God made us and all our skills to fit into His divine plan. To work with our skills without His plan can never be completely satisfying. But if we understand where we fit in the Creator's plan for mankind, and for our time, then we can gain a true vision and find lasting fulfillment.

> Then Jesus said to His disciples, "If anyone would come after Me, he must deny himself and take up his cross and follow Me. For whoever wants to save his life will lose it, but whoever loses his life for Me will find it. What good will it be for a man if he gains the whole world, yet forfeits his soul?"
> —Matthew 16:24-26

The Lord claims His right to be the master of our lives. There isn't room enough for two behind the steering wheel. If we decide to be in charge and try to drive on the narrow road with our natural abilities, we will experience a wreck. But if we let Him be Lord and He directs everything in our lives according to His will, then He gets us to the right place in the right time, according to His plans. And when we are in the right place at the right time, our skills and gifts will be there enabling us to work, making us master craftsmen, like Paul (1 Cor. 3:10). The only thing necessary is to deny ourselves the place at the wheel.

Let me add another thought. It is better to miss out on experimenting with one of our skills, rather than to miss out on God's will for our lives. There are things about ourselves that we will not understand on this side of heaven. For this short time on earth, we can comfort ourselves with the truth that we are wonderfully made, and God takes pleasure in us. We can make Him laugh for joy by how willingly we walk with Him.

CONSIDERING A GIRL NAMED MARY

Life is not fair, but God is good. Even in the *good old days*, labor for one's own family was hard and unending. From the time God cursed the ground because of sin, Adam and Eve found that life would be difficult. But in the hard work, God also decided to bless the faithful man and woman with joy and satisfaction.

> So I saw that there is nothing better for a man than to enjoy his work, because that is his lot.
> —Ecclesiastes 3:22

But, as we have found so many times before, culture works contrary to this, influencing our attitudes and thinking more than we realize. The old sinful nature operates to satisfy his appetites (Gal. 5:19) and proclaims his rights for convenience, leisure, and entertainment. The more he gets, the more he demands. If he is let loose, he will soon be found involved in gluttonous self-worship, where his desires and wants are the center of his world, and woe on anybody who stands in his way! Children do stand in the way. They are real culprits in destroying adult leisure time, entertainment, and adult tasks. And that's why we need to say, "Lord, let them come."

Consider a girl named Mary. You could say that God was not fair to Mary. She was an unmarried girl, full of dreams. God intercepted those dreams so that one small baby boy (the Son of God) could be born. Mary would never be the same. But because she loved God, she allowed her dreams to change to fit the new circumstances.

Life does not turn out the way I want. However hard I would try to control life, things still happen. Then I remember that everything happens because God has a plan for me, and He is bigger than I. Oh, to learn Mary's heart attitude; to fit into His plan, and not try to fit Him into mine. To live with hands open to Him and not with clenched fists resenting what He brings my way and beating my fists against all unexpected changes. *Lord, may it be unto me according to Your Word.* Is it fair that God imposes His will on us when we are not willing or ready? No, God is not fair because He is good.

Lord Jesus, this one grace is needed in my life: to walk in Your plan, and to work joyfully while You hand life to me. To happily surrender and eagerly receive that which You bring. My heart is desperately wayward, complaining like an Israelite in the desert, while You prepare a feast. Transform my heart to willingly walk in Your ways and Your light. Forgive me and cleanse me from this sin. And then teach me to feast with You.

Beating the Odds

Do not love the world or anything in the world. If anyone loves the world, the love of the Father is not in him... The world and its desires pass away, but the man who does the will of God lives forever.

—1 John. 2:15, 17

Today's Challenge

"I have some good news and some bad news," the doctor greeted his patient who woke up after surgery. "Which do you want to hear first?"

"Tell me the bad news first," answered the patient.

"The bad news is that we by mistake amputated the wrong leg." Then the doctor added quickly, "But the good news is, we've found out that we don't need to amputate your other leg after all."

I have some good news and some bad news, too! The bad news is that today's world does not make it easier for us to obey the Lord in receiving and rearing children. We are facing unique challenges as Christian couples, and we are lacking some of the support earlier generations relied on to fulfill their tasks. Sorry to say this, but it is not an easy road if we decide to take it. The good news is, it will be worth it!

Few people ever regret having children, and those who have their eyes set on a heavenly reward find their present inconveniences to be *light and momentary* (2 Cor. 4:17-18). Whether we raise strong-willed, obstinate die-hards, or gentle, sensitive little angels, we will receive a reward that far surpasses any hardship we experience in our tasks of child rearing. (For me the mere act of surrendering my body to Him brings peace, joy and health!) How easy it is to persevere in our tasks when we know without a doubt that we are on the right track!

"My food," said Jesus, "is to do the will of Him who sent Me and to finish His work."
—John 4:34

Our main objective in our lives as Christians is to become like Jesus, to learn what His will is for us and to complete it. Whatever the world says or offers, our fulfillment is found in nothing and in no one else!

This chapter has been dedicated to exploring and answering today's special circumstances and challenges. The main challenges that will be addressed are: family expectations, shame projection from culture and dysfunctional church care. May the following information help keep us alert and sound, in body, mind, spirit, and our legs to be intact and on firm ground!

When Your Spouse Doesn't Agree

A husband and wife do not always simultaneously come to the conclusion that God should be in control of their family size, and that can lead to a lot of frustration. If you are in that position, let me encourage you.

I don't think many people living in the Western culture would be able to have a good perspective on child bearing or the rearing of children if God's Spirit didn't overhaul their hearts. If you have been able to understand and give your body over to the Lord for these purposes, it is a sign that the Holy Spirit has been at work in you. And if He did that in you, it was because He wanted to bring your whole family to a new understanding. You can be sure He will be working in your husband or wife. Pray until you see it realized, and trust God to do His work in the right time and way. You cannot change your mate's heart, but you can be a change agent through your prayers and support.

As a woman speaking to women: if you are the one who desires more children, but your husband does not, please remain under his leading. He is responsible for his family before God, and you are free from any guilt if he decides contrary to what you believe is right. Continue to lay your requests before the Lord until He brings about change and support your husband. He carries a lot on his shoulders.

There are ways to win a spouse over without nagging or arguing. It is done simply by looking to Jesus. Our marriages are to reflect His relationship with the church. A man loves his wife and woos her to himself by his gentle leading. He does not force his will, but waits and woos. A wife wins her husband's ear and attention by her reverent life and by how she respects and prefers him (Eph. 5:22-33; 1 Peter 3:1-4). For such an intimate act as is required to become carriers of life, it takes two committed hearts before the Lord to fulfill His purposes. May God grant you the joy of such unity!

LIFE IN THE SEVENTIES

What do we do when a husband and wife are in agreement but their parents are not? Let's think for a little while about that. The Bible tells us,

> Train a child in the way he should go, and when he is old he will not turn from it.
> —Proverbs 22:6

Just as we train our children, we were also trained by our parents. To help us understand how and with what attitudes they trained us, we need to take a look at the culture they lived in when we were born. We can then evaluate our current situation, and know what we have inherited from them, either good or bad.

There have been drastic changes taking place in our culture over the last hundred years, especially concerning the attitudes toward children and family life. Young couples will find that their parents were born and raised in the aftermath of the feministic battle, when the West was already reshaped to fit the new attitude. I believe the seventies represented the peak of acceptance of the new ideology; most women went to work, babies were bottle-fed and sent to daycare, career was in, homemaking was out. There was no room for disagreement without a cultural bashing.

This generalized view of the seventies helps us to realize that the age in which our parents lived out their young years was very rigid. It regulated common man's dreams down to earthly, tangible successes, and it set up perimeters for what success should look like and having a small, groomed family was one of them. It became such an ingrained norm that it somehow slipped into the church and became accepted as the way to live the Christian life as well (and has remained there uncontested!). When it comes to understanding our own choices for having or not having children, we might unwittingly be paying homage to an ungodly, fleeting era of the West rather than paying attention to the directions of Almighty God.

If our parents unknowingly choose the wrong roads because of their worldview, we will serve both them and the Lord best by redeeming the future through understanding and obedience. God wants us to have all the children He gives us; He wants them welcomed, cared for, reared, and trained. Can we even begin to fathom what power He would bestow on our children if they rose up as one and offered themselves unreservedly to Him? But I pray they will be the ones who will see Him come back in glory, having completed the task He gave.

When I was in my teens, I watched the signs of the age and was excited at the thought that I might be in the last generation before His return. However, with these last eight years of marriage and seeing our children born and watching the Lord move, I become more and more convinced that it will be our children's generation who will play the greater part. Whether they are the last generation or not, I cannot say, but I believe the Lord wants to say to all of us who are married and in our child-bearing years, that the time is drawing short. This is not a time for procrastination or for divided interests. This is the time of bringing forth and training and equipping the next generation. The Church today needs to take on the role of Elizabeth, who was barren for a long time, but whom the Lord visited and granted conception in order to raise up John the Baptist – a generation whose whole identity is wrapped up in fulfilling the work of God and preparing for His return. Are you willing to play the role of Elizabeth, dear ones, for His sake?

Family Expectations

Once I talked with a neighbor lady who had three smaller children. She had become a believer not many years earlier, but her family was not Christian. As I shared my desire for children with her, she confided that she wanted more too. But for her it was almost an impossible dream, not because of her husband, but because of her parents! In their eyes, three children had to be more than enough and the woman feared what they would say if she were to become pregnant again. Her situation is far from uncommon. Because of the seventies and all its one-sided propaganda for small families, it is so hard for many of our parents today to believe that a big family actually could be a blessing, especially within their own families.

I was blessed to be born into a family that continued to grow in the seventies and all the way into the nineties! We were the oddballs in town, and it didn't hurt us a bit. (I am actually thankful for it. We became next to immune to cultural pressure).

Do You Dare Trust God for Your Family Size?

Unfortunately, my grandmother was embarrassed by our numbers, and we heard her say after every young sibling's arrival: "Well, now it is all done, I hope." But she never saw the end of the line; four more were born after she passed away. She herself had carried four children, and as the wife of a priest in the Swedish State Church, they received a special visit and correction from higher authorities, declaring that having many children was not a good testimony! The general feeling was that if you had many children, it showed your lack of godly self control. This must have hurt deeply because however much she loved and helped us all, it was still difficult for her to accept her son having so many children.

So we face the first hurdle of modern time. A hundred years ago a large family was generally counted as a blessing. Young families could grow and count on the support and encouragement of their extended families. Times have changed and so have our attitudes. There are thousands of beautiful exceptions, but the general trend has turned toward material prosperity, not physical. Most of my friends and acquaintances were advised by their parents to pursue careers before marriage. Once they were married, they were advised to wait some years before starting a family so that they could finish their studies and establish their marriages and finances. Although the securing of work and completing studies can be good things (please hear me; I am not against education!), they have been glorified too highly. Riches and knowledge are often real hindrances in our pursuit of godliness, and they do bring with them many temptations (1 Tim. 6:6-10; 1 Cor. 1:19-31). Having children and grandchildren, on the other hand, is a great reward from the Lord for any man or woman. If parents advise their children toward career rather than family, then they have lost sight of a very important and blessed part of life.

TOO CLOSE OR TOO FAR AWAY

Call it a paradox or a balancing act, there are challenges in maintaining appropriate boundaries with our parents when we begin raising our own offspring. Some parents find it hard to let go of their grown children and they become closely involved and assume authority.

> For this cause a man shall leave his father and his mother, and shall cleave to his wife; and they shall become one flesh.
> —Genesis 2:24

When God puts two people together in marriage, they become their own decision making entity. The mother of the husband has, throughout history, had a special sense of ownership and the right to tell the wife how to care for him. In Eastern countries today, it is common practice that the couple lives with his parents rather than by themselves. It has led scores of young wives to a bitter and unhealthy existence. But even here in the West, a husband and wife must know how to form decisions away from parental intervention. It is the only way they will be able to grow strong and confident in what the Lord directs them to do. In the end, they are the ones who will be held responsible for how they have functioned as God's stewards. It is better for them to be approved by God than by their parents.

There is a paradox here. On the one hand, we see that couples need space to make decisions and follow through on them without parental intervention (specifically when it comes to trusting God for their family size). However, we find that once they have made their decision they will need plenty of help and encouragement. This entails another challenge of the modern world. In our grandparents' or great-grandparents' time, most families lived relatively close together. Urbanization has changed that. Grandparents may now live on the other side of town, the other side of the state, the other side of America or even on the other side of the world! Many of the close-knit family ties that characterized the older generations have given way to today's fast-paced lifestyles. Where do we find support in our roles as parents when our own families are far away or are not stepping into their role of nurturing? We are about to find an answer!

DYSFUNCTIONAL CHURCH CARE

We live in exciting times. Because my husband and I belong to a church that has decided to go all out for the Lord Jesus, we keep seeing God's work manifested in our midst. Ever since I began reading the New Testament and the accounts of the Apostles, I have had a hunger to see the church move in the same passion and power as it did in those early days. I see Him do this now, in these days – He is restoring functions to the church that have been forgotten or neglected for a long time. One church function that has been lost since the feminist movement took over and women abandoned the home as their work place has been the role of the *older woman*. It has little to do with age, and everything to do with her faithfulness in executing the Lord's will in daily life. I believe that a lot of the challenges I have been describing so far in this chapter can be overcome if we rediscover the *older woman* role and put it into practice.

Why put such an emphasis on women and their role in the home? Simply because the woman is the one who has been deceived the most. As I said in the first chapter, it seemed the man's place was the best one and she keeps on wanting it. A friend of mine confessed that she thought a woman would make a much better man than a man! But in the end, that's not the point. The point is, for what reason did the Lord create women? When we discover that and do what the Creator equipped us to do, then we find fulfillment and real joy. The question is not, "What can I do with my life?" but rather, "What am I supposed to do with my life?" The first question leads to a million alternatives; the second to the will of God.

An older woman is one who has lived her life in the will of God. Titus 2:3-5 describes her as one who is able to teach what is good. She becomes what the married young women need: someone whom they can go to for advice and accountability. I wish I had an older woman in my early days of marriage when I was floundering and trying to make heads and tails of all the sensitive issues that came up. It would have helped me to realize the truth that we need to be trained to become godly wives and mothers; it doesn't just happen with time.

When we read the Titus passage mentioned above, we find that a young married woman needs an older woman to train her in:

- How to love her husband. (It doesn't just happen! It takes training!)
- How to love her children. (We can't rely on maternal instinct or disposition.)
- How to be self-controlled and pure. (If we don't understand why God put us in our specific positions and do not have His purposes in mind, it will be easy to lose ourselves in useless pursuits or fantasies at home where no one sees us)
- How to be busy at home. (Having children will take care of that!)
- How to be kind. (You will discover it doesn't come naturally after the second child.)
- How to be subject to her husband (How I cried and fought for headship before I began

to understand this hard concept and I'm still learning!)

This is refreshing. The Lord knows marriage and parenting are two tough jobs with a lot of character refining taking place. With this in mind, He enlists older women to be His ambassadors to young families and especially to the young wife who frequently feels confused, overwhelmed and tossed about emotionally with pregnancies and growing responsibilities. The older woman acts as a second anchor, providing additional stability alongside the husband (1 Peter 3:7). I believe a husband similarly can seek counsel among the elders of the church. They are men who have proven themselves to be faithful and trustworthy. If the elders went through their parenting years whole-heartedly, they will have a wealth of wisdom to share. (See more in chapter four under *Competent to Minister*.)

COMMIT AND CONNECT

We've been looking in all directions in this chapter—first at the modern world today, then at the seventies, and then to the present and what God wants to do through reviving the role of the older woman. Many things have gone wrong in the past and many things have left us slightly crippled in following the Lord's directives for raising a family today. The good news keeps surfacing as well. If you are new to all these ideas about allowing God to be in control of your family size then you will be surprised to know how many families already live this way and how fast the numbers are growing.

Two words are vital here, commit and connect. When we see and understand God's plan for the family, we will need to come to terms with how we will respond. Forming a firm conviction and a commitment to the Lord to fulfill His purposes for you and your descendants will keep you on a steady course. (You will find a prayer of commitment in Appendix A, for your reference.) Next, connect with like-minded people so that you will have support and encouragement. God is not intending His work to be a drag but an exceeding joy. There is strength in numbers! For this purpose, there are resources in the back of this book to help you and I pray you will be able to find connections through them.

Finally, take heart and search for elders and older women who have been faithful in the raising of their families, and ask their advice. Take time to get to know them. If you cannot find a virtuous person with this background, study the good women (or men) around you and make note of what they do really well and allow that to be an example to follow. My *older woman* who pushed me out of immaturity happens to be three women. A Pakistani old woman who was full of the Holy Spirit; a German missionary lady who was ruthlessly honest with herself and in dealing with sin; and an American lady who in her brokenness was touched by the Lord and ministers healing to others. Though I haven't seen any of them for years, their lives transformed me. There are several good ministries that have sprung up to serve mothers who choose to stay at home with the purpose of helping them to gain perspective and vision for their task. You will find this information in the section titled *Resources*.

SHAME PROJECTION

When you begin your road toward having a larger family, the world will give you a bashing for your views. Larger families testify that the hardest time is during the transition, when you are neither a small family, nor very big. People just do not understand your desire to have children or know what to think of you. As you continue in faith, you may be surprised by the fierce animosity or the harsh judgments you encounter. Although this is not always the case – you will find encouragement in the public place as well – the real test comes when you are judged or ridiculed. Would you know how to react under such pressure?

Friends, we are on a mission. The world system that surrounds us is built on half truths and twisted thinking. We are commissioned to expose them and uphold God's truth.

> The weapons we fight with are not the weapons of the world. On the contrary, they have divine power to demolish strongholds. We demolish arguments and every pretension that sets itself up against the knowledge of God, and we take

captive every thought to make it obedient to Christ.
—2 Corinthians 10:4-5

Do not be overcome by evil, but overcome evil with good.
—Romans 12:21

This is the very thing we need to do. If people blurt out unkind, untrue, or perverse remarks about children or the family, we need to speak up. We are ambassadors for Christ and we are responsible for upholding that which is precious to Him.

It can be a real sport, knowing how to answer people in a way that will impact them. Since we are called to be His witnesses, let's consider some good and simple ways to declare that children are good gifts from a good God and that He would never give us too many of them. How would you answer the following (often heard) remarks?

1. "You've got your hands full!"
2. "Don't you know where they come from?"
3. "Maybe it's time to slow down."
4. "I could never handle that many kids."
5. "Glad it's you and not me."
6. "Are they all yours?"
7. "How many are you planning to have?"
8. "So many boys - are you working on it so you can have a girl next time?"
9. "How do you stand it?"
10. "Tell your husband (or wife) to slow down."

You can probably think of a hundred funny replies in less than an hour. The point is not so much what we say, but how we say it. I pray the Lord will make us able to seize the opportunities to witness powerfully every time. Here are a few thoughts on why these remarks are potentially harmful and how we can answer them:

1. *"You've got your hands full!"* It is such a common way of exclaiming surprise, shock, pleasure, mockery, etc, that it is the underlying remark that needs to be addressed. If you sense surprise, you could say: "Yes, they are full of good things!" Shock: "No, I think I could fit a few more!" Pleasure: "Thank you; they are God's blessings to me." Mockery: "Better full than empty."
2. *"Don't you know where they come from?"* Clear ignorance of Who is in control of conception and birth. "Yes, they come from the hand of God, the Giver of all good things." (If there is time: "My spouse and I are willing to receive them as fast as He sends them, though.")
3. *"Maybe it's time to slow down."* Trying to interfere with the plans and purposes of God for your family. Simply: "No, praise God, not yet." Or longer, "God has blessed me with a great body. It is doing exactly what He tells it to do. So will I." If time: "Don't worry, when the Lord has given me as many as He has planned, He will slow me to a stop."

4. *"I could never handle that many kids."* Belief that you have to have special skills to be a good parent. "I didn't think I could either. But with God all things are possible and it is fun!" (If time, share how your relationship with God helps you in your task of parenthood.) You could also tackle the misconception that the workload doubles for every additional child – it is not true!
5. *"Glad it's you and not me."* Disdain for the blessing of God. When a man blurted this out to my husband once, Jeff gratefully replied, "I'm glad it's me too."
6. *"Are they all yours?"* It can be a simple question, shock or admiration. If it is said in a disapproving or negative way, the answer might be a simple, "Yes, they sure are!" but with a show of how glad you are for your children.
7. *"How many are you planning on having?"* You can answer the misguided conclusion that all people "plan" children rather than receiving them by saying, "I plan on receiving all the children God gives me." To respond to the question that expresses disapproval, a lighthearted comment can act as a positive thought provoker. "A dozen more, at least!" "My husband would like a soccer team." Or kindly, "I am praying for more. Children are a blessing."
8. *"So many boys - are you working on it so you can have a girl next time?"* Misconception that

children are only welcome if they fulfill the parents' wishes. "No, we are 'working on it' so that we will not miss out on any of the great things God wants to do in our family. Another boy would be just as welcome."

9. *"How do you stand it?"* Misconception spread through propaganda, that staying at home with children is a drag and equals a less fulfilling life. "It would be quite tough, if I didn't have my children to cheer me up! They really bring life with them!" (If time, share how the joy of having children far outweighs the trouble of maintenance.)

10. *"Tell your husband (or wife) to slow down."* Throwing blame at your absent spouse, pretending to support you as a victim. "Sir/Ma'am, me and my husband/wife have decided together to trust God for our family size. If you have trouble with that, I refer you to Him."

SAFE IN HIM

Take some time to reflect on culture. With a massive flood of opinion coming towards you, what do you do? Agree with it and be pleasantly swept along with the stream or disagree and swim against the current. That's what God is asking us to do. To live in the world but not be of the world. Like little specks of light in a dark, dark night. We become vessels through which the Morning Star, Jesus, shines His heavenly light into the earthly chaos.

Do You Dare Trust God for Your Family Size?

When we have our eyes on Jesus and on our future hope, we do not fear the intimidation and threats against us. We know without a doubt that we can carry out the Lord's plans for us. He will grant us the grace, the strength and the protection we need.

> I can do everything [God asks me to do] through Him who gives me strength.
> —Philippians 4:13

The medical field will discourage us from having children with their statistics, the culture will intimidate, our own family may pressure, our upbringing and education may dissuade us—all to make us comply with the given norm. Yet when He calls us to do a work for Him, He delivers us from our fears and inadequacies and brings us to faith. We can trust Him!

Sure, having children and rearing them can be dangerous to our health. It can also be tiring, money-stretching and very humbling. But if that is His will for us then there is no safer place on earth for us to be. No better place, no place more satisfying, no place better for character-building, and no place so ultimately good (Rom. 8:28). Corrie ten Boom wrote, "If you look at the world, you will be distressed; if you look within, you will be depressed; but if you look at Christ, you will be at rest."

Rest in the hand of the Almighty, dear friend. He does not make mistakes.

Chapter Seven

Positively Yes!

Has not the LORD made them one? In flesh and Spirit they are His. And why one? Because He was seeking a godly offspring.

—Malachi 2:15

The Birth of a Vision

Affirming children and giving God full control in family planning is the beginning of understanding the purposes God has in mind for His people. The Bible verse that keeps pressing on my heart is Malachi 2:15. God is looking for a generation that will be set apart before birth – even conception – for His purposes. It will be a generation that has been trained in godliness, is strong in His Word, and empowered by a spirit of willingness for sacrifice. This is even more pressing as we approach the end of the ages. Psalm 110 speaks of the Father preparing the time for His Son to rule the world,

> The LORD says to my Lord; "Sit at my right hand until I make your enemies a footstool for your feet." The LORD will extend your mighty scepter from Zion; you will rule in the midst of your enemies. Your troops will be willing [will sacrifice themselves willingly] on your day of battle.
> —Psalm 110:1-3

Even now, we see prophecies being fulfilled as the world heads toward the end times. We must all be ready to sacrifice, but even more so, we need to raise up a generation that will be discerning of the times and fearless for the Lord. To prepare the time of handing over our torch to our sons and daughters is one of the most important tasks we will ever have, since the way our children play a part in impacting the world for Jesus will one day be our crown and glory. If we have trained a troop of children, the impact and the reward will be so much greater.

As we enter into a covenant with the Lord God to have children according to His timing, there is one more thing needed. As we willingly learn to receive the little ones into our families, we also must learn to take up the task of committing them to Him for service. You might think, *How can I force my choices onto my children? They need to choose their path for themselves.* But you know what? Whether you try or not, you will by just being their parent influence them in some direction. God stands behind the word *family* - it has derived its name from Him (Eph. 3:15). So you carry, whether you are a believer or not, the image of God to your children. To lead them in the way they should walk is the very best thing you can do for them. He who is not led through childhood will not experience freedom, but confusion; how much better for them to know that God created them for a purpose greater than they can imagine! (Ps. 40:5) By knowing this truth they will seek to know their purposes, and not settle for a life without it. They will be a people passionate to do God's will like Jesus (John 6:38; 14:30-31). May we, as parents, not be a hindrance, but a help for them to know these things!

An Army of Children

Jesus surrounded Himself not with hundreds of disciples, but with twelve as His core group. For three years, while heavily involved in His earthly ministry, He stayed focused on the task of training His chosen friends. His little band of followers, empowered by the Holy Spirit, changed the world. Love, attention, ministry, training, discipleship, and companionship with the Master changed the lives of these rugged men. They became willing vessels for their Lord. They were not special or greater than any other humans. But they seized hold of what they had learned and rendered themselves willing, and God used them.

It is the same for any of us.

> For the eyes of the LORD range throughout the earth to strengthen those whose hearts are fully committed to Him.
> —2 Chronicles 16:9

The Lord is looking for people who are willing to be used for His purposes. Modern culture has molded people who are not willing to commit or sacrifice, but instead, seek self-fulfillment. Many of us are so inundated with this that we struggle greatly to keep hold of what God has for our lives. Our children, if trained in God's Word and firsthand experiencing God's leading in their lives, do not need to carry as great a struggle. God intends to make our children stronger and better equipped than we are!

> Hear, O Israel: The LORD our God, the LORD is one. Love the LORD your God with all your heart and with all your soul and with all your

> strength. These commandments that I give you today are to be upon your hearts. Impress them on your children. Talk about them when you sit at home and when you walk along the road, when you lie down and when you get up.
> —Deuteronomy 6:4-7

Even with very small children, you will notice how training guides their decisions and actions. They are easily molded and capable of learning many things in a day (just look at their language learning!). Everything that is taught over and over in a home will have an impact for good or bad. If you constantly show gratefulness for God's provision, your children will soon understand that God is the supplier of all needs. If you stress obedience and respect for authorities, they will know it is important to understand God-given positions and roles. If you show and speak of the love of Jesus, you warm their hearts to receive Him. If you pray with them and for them, and remind them when the answer comes, that it was an *answer* and not just coincidence, they will learn to trust God.

Many believers received Christ as their personal Savior before the age of fifteen. You know, God could have chosen to have humans step into history fully grown up and skipped over the childhood part. But He didn't. Somehow He delighted in the formative years and in the hearts and minds of children. If they learn about Him, they are so naturally drawn to Him as their Heavenly Father. They trust Him.

There is so much more that could be said, but I trust the examples are enough to encourage you. The reward comes every time we see our children respond to our training. The apostle John wrote,

> I have no greater joy than to hear that my children are walking in the truth.
> —3 John 1:4

And the Lord charges both fathers and mothers to do this training of their children (Proverbs 6:20-23). Oh, that we might commit to train our children for the Lord! If twelve disciples could impact the world, how much more can an army of children do!

THE BOOTH EXAMPLE

At the moment the missionary force is lacking in numbers and in power. The common plea for help in missions awareness meetings has been, "Pray, go, give…" Many times there has been such a desperate need for laborers, for prayer and funds that it has pushed out the need of long-term planning, but that is the one other thing that is needed. On the frontlines are those people who pray, become laborers, and give their all. Those who have children and rear them for God's purposes are the folks behind the scenes who help replenish the mission workforce. The fruit of the first group is seen now; the fruit of the second will be revealed in fifteen years.

Positively Yes!

I believe this is one of God's answers for reaching the lost, though it has been forgotten these last decades. If we fulfill the first commandment – receive our offspring and raise up the new generation – we help fulfill the last commission. We would do well to remember from what kind of families some of the faithful of old emerged, and what they themselves accomplished. John Wesley was from a family of nineteen children. He became a "burning" preacher, thanks to his mother's choice of teaching and spending time with each of her children. Another great impact was made by the Booth clan.

> William Booth (1829-1912) founded The Salvation Army with his wife Catherine in 1865, in their home country of England. As a zealous evangelist, his passion for the lost was especially for those who were outcasts of the established church. His whole life can be summed up in his own words: "Go for souls, and go for the worst!"

> Even though William and Catherine were heavily involved in evangelism and helping the poor, they never forgot the importance of training up their own eight children in the ways of the Lord. The children learned early in life that they were expected to obey their parents, and that life was no game. One son said, "None of us grew up slackers; none of us played with life."

> While the Booth home was well disciplined, it was also affectionate, and in the early days

> William was often found wrestling the children on the floor, or letting the little girls play with his hair as he read a book. Emma, speaking about her mother, said, "She was the light of our home, the inspiration of our childhood, the ideal of our ambitions, the repository of our confidences, the guardian angel of our souls, and the beacon of our lives as we sailed earth's sea towards the same blissful Harbor in which she has dropped anchor forever."
>
> William and Catherine Booth dedicated their children to the same work God called them to - loving a lost and hurting world to Jesus. They were not disappointed by the results. All their children were workers in God's Kingdom, taking the Gospel to many nations including India, France, Switzerland, and the United States.[23]

Though we sometimes hear of William Booth and his work, we seldom hear of his children. Yet, I am sure in his eyes and in God's, raising his children was as great an investment. Though his own impact was immeasurable, the arrows from his quiver were hurled 'far beyond his reach', as they spread around the globe proclaiming the risen Lord. William was a wise investor, sowing both into the present and into the future.

Say Yes!

The Word is full of the Lord's thoughts and desires for children. The scriptures we have been studying in this book function as witnesses to His person and character, and let us know that He is trustworthy in all things. We can trust Him. Whatever we hand over to Him to care for He will never mess up; whether it be our marriage, our family size, our health, or our work. If we are in control, we surely will mess up! If we truly believe that He is Who He says He is, we can stake our lives on Him, and let go of our control (and the fear of losing control).

It's as simple as this: say yes. When you were saved, you gave Him your heart and the control over your life, as best as you knew how. Now, give Him control over your children; the ones you have, the ones you desire, the ones He desires. Let go of them. Before you can receive, you must let go. Release all responsibility that comes with having children. Lay all responsibility for all outcomes – your children's health and well-being, all pregnancies, all conceptions, all deaths – onto Him. He is strong enough to carry it, and you will be free from all performance, guilt or anger when things happen differently than you imagined. Proclaim Him good in all His works, the one who causes all things to work for the good of those who love Him.

Proclaim His lordship over your reproductive organs, and ask Him to place His blessing on them. Pray for your children, for those you have and the ones He will give; your agreement to have them and raise them for Him will bless and free them to become who God calls them to be, and your prayers will pave the way and guard them from Satan's attacks. (You can be sure of this: if you dedicate your children to fulfill the purposes of God, they will be on Satan's black-list - it's really long.) Release control, receive the blessing, accept the gift, thank the Giver, deliver the child, bring up the child, release him or her for service, and look for your reward. Say yes.

> And whoever welcomes a little child like this in my name welcomes me.
> —Matthew 18:5

Yes to Training

We as parents have the responsibility and the challenge to help our children grow to a place where they can start learning directly from the Lord, and become powerful agents for God's kingdom. What exactly should we do for our children? The Lord will lay on your hearts some things stronger than other things, depending on you and your children's ministries before Him. The list below is in no way comprehensive but is here to trigger ideas for your family.

1. Imprint God's Word on your children's hearts (Deut. 6:4-7).
2. Live as examples of Spirit-filled and transparent lives (they will quickly detect and hate hypocrisy).

3. Discipline them, so they will be receptive to obeying the Lord when He speaks.
4. Help them put love, unselfishness, repentance and forgiveness into practice.
5. Continually present the gospel to them in many different ways.
6. Teach them to distinguish right from wrong, help form their conscience, and teach them how to stand against ungodly cultural influences or peer pressure.
7. Let them understand that the invisible, higher reality is to be set above the visible and material.
8. Teach them to value what God values.
9. Let them know that they were born for specific purposes, and encourage them to seek until they find out what those are. You could do them no greater service.
10. Love your children unconditionally, and take time to listen to them.

The following great things will happen because of your devotion to the Lord in raising your children in a godly manner:

Your children will pass on the knowledge of God both in their generation and in the next. Your sowing will reap a great harvest.

> Since my youth, O God, You have taught me, and to this day I declare Your marvelous deeds. Even when I am old and gray, do not forsake me, O

> God, till I declare Your power to the next generation, Your might to all who are to come.
> —Psalm 71:17-18

Your children will become mighty for Him.

> Praise the LORD. Blessed is the man who fears the LORD, who finds great delight in His commands. His children will be mighty in the land; the generation of the upright will be blessed.
> —Psalm 112:1-2

You pass on a mantle of righteousness to your children and grandchildren, because of God's love and favor on you.

> But from everlasting to everlasting the LORD's love is with those who fear Him, and His righteousness with their children's children - with those who keep His covenant and remember to obey His precepts.
> —Psalm 103:17-18

May the Lord put such a stamp of approval on the children you raise!

Yes to the Season of Childbearing

Say yes to the God-given season of childbearing by taking your hand away from control over your reproduction and handing it back to the Creator. If the Lord grants you the faith, ask Him to bless you to the brim of His perfect will for you as a family. Then set your house in order and wait. Your situation will be so unique; I would love to hear how the Lord works His miracle in your home. Let me share how the season started up for us.

Six weeks after our wedding we became pregnant with our first baby. Though dazed, we were still very excited at the thought of having a baby. As the due date approached, we watched videos on how I should breathe through the contractions, and it gave advice to my husband on how to support me. In my state of innocence, I decided that I should try to impact the nurses by my calm appearance and the memorizing of Bible verses through labor (go ahead and laugh, mothers). I gathered my verses. Eleven days overdue, the water finally broke at midnight after returning from a late Bible study. Excitement deprived us of sleep for the rest of the night, as we were placed in a small country hospital and roamed the corridors to start up contractions. At noon we were still not progressing, and they decided to induce. In a few hours, the pain shot up to levels I found almost unbearable. My zealous husband kept counting to three and trying to keep my attention on him rather than the pain. The memory verses were untouched by my bedside, while I wondered where God was hiding. It felt as if I was walking through the valley of death. After an eternity of pain that lasted until late afternoon, my firstborn son was born. That night I fell into an exhausted sleep, but woke up later in the night by a baby crying in another room.

Do You Dare Trust God for Your Family Size?

Painfully, I got up to see how my baby, Josef, was doing (and to check if the nurses knew what they were doing!). I stood peering at him through the glass, and a pain of another kind shot through me. I was his mother. He was my son, and I loved him. I forgot the pain of delivery and realized it was truly worth it. The reward was so great.

I am sure many of you can understand how I felt. My story is not as dramatic as many of yours would be. It is simply the introduction I had to practically understand and appreciate what Jesus went through for me (on a small scale!) and that He really thought it worthwhile. Now I am so glad to be a woman. I am glad that I can go through delivery, and get to know my Lord's pain in a way He has only granted mothers. And I rejoice even more when delivery is over, and I hold that sweet reward in my arms—new life.

Because of sin, God added pain to childbearing. It was to stand as a sign for all time and for all generations that sin brings pain. But it also pointed to Jesus, the man who was willing to shoulder our sin and die with it, to bring about a great delivery for us all. In pain, we give birth to our children, and in pain, God birthed the church through Jesus Christ with new life for us all. It is sweet that Jesus knows our mother role so intimately!

Barbara Nelson, a mother of many, wrote this reminder to women, "The childbearing years are not forever." We tend to think of the future as one long eternity, stretching endlessly in front of us. But even the secular world is realizing that the baby making machine (the woman's body) has been given set limits to its fruitfulness. Even more, so should we who belong to the Lord, recognize that the window of childbearing will someday close. On August 13, 2001, the Newsweek cover article was, "The Truth about Fertility - Why more doctors are warning that Science can't beat the biological clock." The article created a great stir among women, especially those in their thirties. For a while, the medical world seemed to promise women that they could focus unhindered on careers for years and still be assured there was time to have children. Instead, many of them found they could not conceive, even with great medical help. The same article also pointed out that medical institutions have become increasingly aware that they have promised women too much and informed too little. "We've fed them a fairy tale."[24] This, too, is a witness to the fact that God is in control of conception, not man and woman. The more a woman gives her body over to having children, the more children He is willing to entrust to her, it seems. When a married woman has refused childbearing for fifteen years, it might be that the Lord has turned His eyes away from her as an eligible mother and is contemplating sending His gifts to other wombs; so she finds herself barren. Repentance and seeking the Lord's face can change that, for He has promised to turn to us if we turn to Him (Zech. 1:3).

It is good to hand over our early years of marriage to the Lord, showing ourselves eager to be blessed with the good gifts of children. I've been in contact with a number of women who experience a time of mourning when entering menopause, and they realize they have seen the end of their line of children. A long season of service is over, and it has, despite hardships, been the most rewarding, most fulfilling and joyful season of most women's lives. Husbands too, will find themselves affected by the transition. Having little children in the house takes a lot of patience and sacrifice, but they also create the pulse of life in the home. Oh, that we would learn to cherish the season of childbearing!

Yes to Love and Service

As a single, I prayed to the Lord to make me the most loving and serving woman I could become. My thoughts were on serving Him as a single, but He chose to work out His answer by giving me a husband and sending me children! I know now that my understanding of love and of true sacrifice was very shallow and opinionated. Instead of the public life of the single woman on the mission field, I found myself almost hidden from sight in the solitude of a home. Who would see my service there? Who, except my husband, would know about my attitudes, moods, or true outpouring of love? I found that my heart was much more inclined to do good if there was some incentive of glory for me, not for my God! True love would have flown freely without a care to who was watching or not. I had asked to become loving. First, I needed to know what love was. And for every father or mother, the gift of parenthood is one of the best catalysts for learning to love well.

Then followed the lesson of service. Elisabeth Elliot wrote in her leaflet *Called to Be Mothers*, "A woman knows, in the deepest regions of her being, that it is this very self-giving for which she was made. Single or married, her level of maturity is measured by how much she gives to others. If she is married, she gives herself to her husband and she receives. If she is a mother, she loses her life in her child and - mysteriously - she *finds* it."

For pregnant women: the Lord is at work day and night in your body and you are serving Him by allowing Him to work in you. You speak a continual, "Yes, Lord!" by simply being and carrying. You live Romans 12:1, offering your body as a sacrifice to the Lord, and He even counts it as worship! One mother said that even if she did nothing else in a day, just being pregnant was a great contribution to life. But as a mother, the tasks of dishwashing, cooking, cleaning, washing clothes, reading for the children, changing diapers, feeding, playing, loving, training, disciplining, teaching, and praying – all is counted as worship if you offer it up to the Lord. You are offering yourself to serve; God is pleased with that sacrifice.

Do not be afraid of the load and responsibility that comes with having children. Do not shrink from the things that will impact you and change you, and that will bring Him joy. I'm not saying there won't be work. There will be a lot of work. But it will be work that counts and builds confidence, character, and fulfillment. Who does not want to say yes to that?

Yes to Looking for a Heavenly Reward

Having children might at times seem like a thankless task. Nevertheless, it will one day be rewarded greatly if carried out diligently. Fathers and mothers alike face the exhaustion from constant giving and not always receiving.

> God is not unjust; He will not forget your work [meaning, those things you did that drained your energy, to serve Him] and the love you have shown Him as you have helped His people and continue to help them. We want each of you to show this same diligence to the very end, in order to make your hope sure. We do not want you to become lazy, but to imitate those who through faith and patience inherit what has been promised.
> —Hebrews 6:10-12

The Lord shows a special tenderness towards the tired mother who has accepted her role as wife (helper), mother, and home manager, and who struggles to know whether her workload and all the practicalities of life really amount to anything significant. Just such a mother is Annette Beasley, a precious woman and mother of many, who wondered this very thing as her responsibilities grew bigger. The Lord then visited her with a powerful revelation from His Word, and now she passes it on to us. This is what she wrote:

How Meditating on God's Word Inspired an Overwhelmed Mother

> Do not store up for yourselves treasures on earth, where moth and rust destroy and where thieves break in and steal. But store up for yourselves treasures in heaven, where moth and rust do not destroy, and where thieves do not break in and steal. For where your treasure is, there your heart will be also.
> —Matt. 6:19

Several years ago after reading this Scripture, I asked God to show me how I could store up for myself treasures in heaven. He gave me a little bit of an answer, about giving to the poor and helping those in need, but I put it on the back burner hoping that God would show me some way that I could practically live out those verses.

How can I practically do this? What can I do that will store up for myself treasures in heaven and thus allow me to obey the command of my Lord?

Years later, after having five children ages eight, five, four, three, one, expecting number six, and home schooling, I found myself feeling inadequate and overwhelmed with the task and demands of motherhood. In desperation I cried out to the Lord, "I can't do this! Please help me. I know this is what You want me to do, but could You please send me some encouragement."

I came across this Scripture

Command those who are rich in this present world not to be arrogant nor to put their hope in wealth, which is so uncertain, but to put their hope in God, who richly provides us with everything for our enjoyment. Command them to do good, to be rich in good deeds, and to be generous and willing to share. In this way they will lay up treasure for themselves as a firm foundation for the coming age, so that they may take hold of the life that is truly life.
—1 Tim. 6:17-19

I paused; there was the answer to the prayer I had offered up years ago! I could lay up treasures in heaven for myself by being rich in good deeds. Now what did that mean for me as a mother? It wouldn't have meant a whole lot except just a few minutes ago I had read the verses in the previous chapter. It all fit together and God gave a revelation to my heart.

In the days of the early church, the church provided for the widows, but before a widow could be put on the list of widows she had to fulfill certain requirements. Three of these requirements are listed in 1 Timothy 5:9-10. It says, *"No widow may be put on the list of widows unless she is over sixty, has been faithful to her husband, and is well known for her good deeds. She is well known for her good deeds, such as bringing up children."*

Bringing up children is a good deed. Bringing up children is a good deed before God. Simply bringing up children is a way that I as a mother can lay up for myself treasures in heaven, where moth and rust will not destroy and where thieves will not break in and steal.

It goes on and says several other things that are listed as good deeds *"...such as bringing up children, showing hospitality, washing the feet of the saints, helping those in trouble, and devoting herself to all kinds of good deeds."* I think these are things that we as wives and mothers should be fully, zealously devoted to. But particularly, I think we need to understand, in our day, that bringing up children is a good deed before God.

If you're a mother with little ones, if you're a mother with children at home, just bringing up those children is in itself a pleasing sacrifice. It is precious; it's a good deed before God. And all the Scriptures that mention doing good, "Be excellent in what is good," or, "Let us not become weary in doing good," or, "Do not forget to do good...for with such sacrifices God is pleased," or, "Commit yourself to your faithful Creator and continue to do good," can apply here. Continue to endure in this challenging area of bringing up children – it is precious in the sight of God.[25]

Thank You, Lord, for this revelation, that You count it a good deed, with an eternal reward waiting, when we bring up our children. Send this truth into the heart of every struggling mother, to steady her against the lies that surround her.

A Full Life

Here we are, at the end of a book that has taken years to write, in between the moves over three continents and the birth of four more children into our family. I am more convinced than ever that we are on the right road when we accept children to come like this, and I stand in awe of the Lord's glory laid down in every individual life. It is an honor to be a parent to the image-bearers of Almighty God, and in years to come I will thank Him again and again that my husband and I decided to walk this road together. (Unlike me, my husband didn't grow up in a large family, yet he is walking forward with us in this. I am so grateful for my God-given match!)

I believe a family full of children experiences a full life. Not necessarily because of their number (any number God chooses will be full), but because of the harmony they live with God's unconditional love and acceptance of life. When every family member is welcomed as part of God's plan, and the parents are resting in His Lordship over their children, home becomes a beautiful place. My husband's favorite Scripture reads, *"Do nothing out of selfish ambition or vain conceit, but in humility consider others better than yourselves. Each of you should look not only to your own interests, but also to the interests of others"* (Phil. 2:3-4). It fits in; as we start seeing God's glory in others, we can even put our children (small as they are for a season) before our own interests and stoop down and serve them. Where selfish desires are put to death and service takes over, there is an abundance of peace and joy, and there the Lord loves to dwell.

"What an ideal picture!" you say. "It sounds too good to be realized." Well, yes, it sounds good, but God is good. He is perfect in all His ways, in His whole person. And when He works in us, He draws out the image of His beloved Son, Jesus. And Jesus is all lovely, all serving, all loving. There is no one like Him, yet we are destined to be like Him! Of course we cannot be all that - but we are enveloped in His grace and mercy until we become like Him. That's our promised destination.

So, how about spreading some of His glory on earth? Take out your calculator and begin dreaming big. If a husband and wife bear eight children for the Lord, and those children have an average family of six each, the family has grown from two to fifty-eight. Then figure out the number by adding the next five generations, say five children per family. If all the children and grandchildren are properly trained and ready to serve the Lord, do you think you would be mighty for the Lord? Would you count your investments worthy of the time and effort, if thirteen grandchildren became missionaries, nine became pastors, and all others made an impact for the Lord in their homes, neighborhoods, and workplaces?

The last century caved in to the deception that a small, monitored family size was the road to success. Many couples got what they thought they wanted; many became rich and materially wealthy, but lost themselves in a shallow lifestyle that brought sorrow rather than happiness. May we be the generation that breaks the trend and sets foot again on the road to a full life, the road that takes us beyond just shunning abortion or liking babies, the road that leads to the very heart of God, the very source of all life. And you know what? If we embrace life, we will find ourselves embracing *Him.*

Square your shoulders, man of God. Be ready for the life of adventure that follows the one who has plunged into the River of God-trust. It will not be easy, but it is what you are really looking for – a life worthy to be lived. Watch as the Lord hands you arrows to sharpen; rejoice as He equips you for battles ahead. You will not be put to shame. (See Psalm 127.)

Dear woman, lift your head and see the one who hands you a crown of honor, who protects you from the storm and gently cares for you while you care for His little ones. Although He leads you through a heavy task, it can not compare to the glory that He has prepared for you. Take heart; let your spirit soar and meet with Him, Who delights in you.

> The thief comes only to steal and kill and destroy;
> I have come that they may have life, and have it to the full.
> —John 10:10

Who, but the Lord, could accomplish such a work in you through a simple, "Yes"?

I Accept My Womb

Dear Father, I come to You in Jesus' name. I confess I have not received my womb as a gift from You. I have ignored the power of my womb and my womanly functions. I repent. Please forgive me and cleanse me in Jesus' name.

Lord, I accept my womb as a gift from You. I accept the way You created me. I embrace it. I want to fulfill Your purposes for me as a woman.

In the name of Your Son, Jesus Christ, I renounce all negative words, even jokingly, that I have spoken about my womb, about menstruation, about pregnancy and about my womanly functions. I renounce any curse that has been placed upon my womb or reproductive organs from my parents, grandparents or great-grandparents on both sides of my family.

I ask that You will now cleanse my womb and cover it with Your blessing. I receive Your blessing in the name of Jesus. Amen.

(From *The Power of Motherhood* study manual by Nancy Campbell)

Releasing Control

Lord, we confess that we have not let You be Lord over our bodies and our fertility. We have misunderstood and neglected Your directions to produce godly offspring according to our ability and Your measure for us. Please forgive us and cleanse us in Jesus' name.

We renounce all negative influence that has had a hold on our minds concerning children and fertility. Whether from culture, friends or family members, we renounce all influence that belittles what You call holy and precious.

We now release our control and hand it over to You. We trust in Your goodness and in Your divine plans for us as a family. We will trust in Your perfect provision—for our health, our finances, for every child You will send us, and for the strength and grace needed for parenthood. We hand over all fear and doubt and ask for a greater measure of faith.

We believe in Your Word, and accept that children are a blessing. We ask now that You honor us with a full quiver, that we will not miss out on any of Your purposes for us and our descendants. Show

Appendix A: I Accept My Womb

us how to steward and train them rightly. Be pleased with this commitment and bless our children, that they may walk in faithfulness and joy before You all their days.

Thank You, Lord, for making us a part of Your plan. We love You and offer ourselves up to You gladly, for the sake of Jesus. Amen.

Resources

Above Rubies – *Strengthening families across the world* (magazine; editress (as she calls herself) Nancy Campbell. It states, "*Above Rubies* is a magazine to encourage women in their high calling as wives, mothers and homemakers. Its purpose is to uphold and strengthen family life and to raise the standard of God's truth in the nation…" It is a non-subscription magazine, supported by contributions. You can be added to the mailing list by writing to *Above Rubies*, PO Box 681687; Franklin, TN 37068-1687, or email nancy@aboverubies.org. This magazine also presents many other materials you can benefit from, such as email groups, books, music, audio messages, family ministries and resources pertaining to topics in the magazine.

The Way Home – Beyond Feminism Back to Reality, Mary Pride. Women who have been taught to think career first will be challenged by this groundbreaking book. Backing up her case she uses a wealth of relevant information linked with Scripture study. She also shares her own conversion from fierce feminist to fulfilled homemaker. As ardently as she once advocated feminism, she now fights against its misconceptions. Crossway Books (a division of Good News Publishers), 1300 Crescent Street; Wheaton, IL 60187

All the Way Home – Power for Your Family to Be Its Best, Mary Pride. The follow-up book to *The Way Home*, Mary Pride moves from facing feminism to laying the foundation for a sound family life, dealing with cultural misconceptions about marriage, sex, having children, how to raise children, and how to be a family. It is a great resource for couples and families today. Crossway Books, 1300 Crescent Street; Wheaton, IL 60187

The Power of Motherhood – What the Word of God says about Mothers (Study manual) Nancy Campbell. An excellent study that brings women face to face with her destiny and purpose, her body and what God designed her for, and what God's Word says. The study both brings out relevant illustrations from real-life experiences and timeless and exciting finds from Bible word studies. It is an excellent and powerful resource, and does well as a woman's group study. From Nancy Campbell you will also find other useful manuals. Write to *Above Rubies*,

Appendix B: Resources

Po Box 681687, Franklin, TN 37068-1687, email nancy@aboverubies.org or see the web page: www.aboverubies.org

A Full Quiver – Family Planning and the Lordship of Christ, Rick and Jan Hess. In a fun and graceful way Rick and Jan tackle the difficult questions around the faith-stretching decision to let God be in control of family planning. The book contains great thought-provoking sections, including history checks (what famous people would not have been born if their parents had had the chance or desire for birth control?) and answering the "infamous twenty questions" about family planning. There is also a section about sterilizations and reversals. $10.00. Write to: Rick and Jan Hess, 7014 Chandler Acres Dr; Bellevue, NE 68147

Endnotes

[1] From her leaflet *Couples Who Choose Not to Have Children*, part of and received from her radio ministry *Gateway to Joy*.

[2] Boyer, *Yes, They're All Ours*, (The Learning Parent, 1994), 118.

[3] A good example is West Germany. Hess, *A Full Quiver* (Hess Publishing, 1990), 75-76. See also Wattenberg, *The Birth Dearth: What Happens When People in Free Countries Don't Have Enough Babies*.

[4] Hess, *A Full Quiver* (Hess Publishing, 1990), 75.

[5] Hess, *A Full Quiver* (Hess Publishing, 1990), quoting *How to Understand Humanism* (Institute in Basic Life Principles, 1983), 70-71.

6. Although most women are called to be wives and mothers, the Lord does call many women to remain single to serve Him in other ways. They are not different from other women, but the Lord chooses to use their maternal heart and willingness to serve in other areas.
7. Pride, *The Way Home* (Crossway Books, 1985), 49.
8. Campbell, *The Power of Motherhood* (Above Rubies, 1996), Chapter Two.
9. It might seem like bad science fiction, but the feminist movement, and in particular those who call themselves ZPG-ers (Zero Population Growth), are working towards laws that equal the one-child law in China. James Weber quotes one major ZPGer as calmly suggesting, "It can be argued that over-reproduction – that is the bearing of more than four children – is a worse crime than most and should be outlawed. One thinks of the possibility of raising the minimum age of marriage, of imposing stiff penalties for illegitimate pregnancy, of compulsory sterilization after a fifth birth." Pride, *The Way Home* (Crossway Books, 1985), 65.
10. Hird, *The Church's Secret Shame* (Christian Reader, July-August 2002).
11. Donna speaks of the atrocities of the partial-birth abortion. You can get a copy of the leaflet *Court Testimony of a Partial-Birth Abortionist* (Leroy Carhart) by requesting

it from Metro Right to Life, 9001 Arbor St, Omaha, NE 68124-2064, ph (402) 399-0299, or by internet www.metrorighttolife.com.

[12] Pride, *The Way Home* (Crossway Books, 1985), 51-56.

[13] Hess, *A Full Quiver* (Hess Publishing, 1990), 121-134.

[14] Hess, *A Full Quiver* (Hess Publishing, 1990), 131.

[15] Hess, *A Full Quiver* (Hess Publishing, 1990), 31-32.

[16] Boyer, *Yes, They're All Ours* (The Learning Parent, 1994), 112-113.

[17] The situation is actually much worse than just ministers using contraceptives within their own families. Christians in humanitarian work many times are active in securing sterilizations or contraceptives for the locals they came to witness to. A recent example is the three Christian aid workers in Yemen who were murdered. The Heartland Gatekeeper reports in June 2003 (Vol. 1, Issue 12), "In April Kamel [the killer] told the court he killed the three workers because he believed they were trying to sterilize Muslim women and convert Muslims to Christianity. An International Mission Board spokesman later told Baptist Press that sterilization procedures would have been done solely with permission of both spouses." So the workers found themselves suffering not only for the

Gospel, but for bringing death rather than life to the people of Yemen.

[18] From her leaflet *Couples Who Choose Not to Have Children*, part of and received from her radio ministry *Gateway to Joy*.

[19] Pride, *All the Way Home* (Crossway Books, 1989), 207-208.

[20] Hess, *A Full Quiver* (Hess Publishing, 1990), 136-137.

[21] *Home Educators' Network NEWS*, Vol. 17, No. 9, June 2003.

[22] Pride, *The Way Home* (Crossway Books, 1985), 48.

[23] Booth, *Training Your Children for Christ*, Last Days Ministries (Pretty Good Printing, 1985).

[24] Quote from Pamela Madsen, executive director of American Infertility Association.

[25] Used with permission.

To order additional copies of

DO YOU DARE TRUST GOD
FOR YOUR FAMILY SIZE?

POSITIVELY YES!

Have your credit card ready and call:

1-877-421-READ (7323)

or please visit our web site at
www.pleasantword.com

Also available at:
www.amazon.com
and
www.barnesandnoble.com

Breinigsville, PA USA
25 October 2010
247988BV00001B/1/A